My *Style,* My *Way*

Top experts reveal how to create yours today

THRIVE
PUBLISHING™

THRIVE Publishing

A Division of PowerDynamics Publishing, Inc.
San Francisco, California
www.thrivebooks.com

ISBN: 978-0-9829419-3-5

Library of Congress Control Number: 2010942846

Printed in the United States of America on acid-free paper.

Table of Contents

Dedication

We dedicate this book to you,
the woman who understands the value
of presenting a stylish image.
We salute you for wanting to
show the world your own unique style
and for being ready to step into
an authentic new vision of yourself—
we celebrate you!

The Co-Authors of *My Style, My Way*

To Ruth Schwartz, with her many years of experience and wisdom, who served as an ongoing guide throughout the project. Your support to our production team and to all of the co-authors is deeply appreciated.

To Tammy Tribble, who brought her creative talent to the cover design, we say thank you for a job well done.

To Barbara McDonald, who brought enthusiasm, creativity, problem-solving and her attention to detail to the book layout, which looks refined and elegant as a result of her efforts.

To Karen Gargiulo and Hester Lox, who brought their keen eyes, their extensive knowledge of punctuation and grammar, and their commitment to clarity—thank you for your support and contribution.

We also acknowledge each other for delivering outstanding information, guidance and advice. Through our work in this book and with our clients, we are committed to enhancing the lives of women through the skills of style. We are profoundly grateful that we get to do work that we love and make a contribution to so many in the process. We do not take our good fortune lightly. We are clear in our mission—to make a genuine contribution to you, the reader. Thank you for granting us this extraordinary opportunity.

The Co-Authors of *My Style, My Way*

Acknowledgements

Gratitude looks good on everyone. Before we share our wisdom and experience with you, we have a few people to thank for turning our vision for this book into a reality.

This book is the brilliant concept of Caterina Rando, an image enthusiast and the founder of THRIVE Publishing™. As a respected business strategist who works with image professionals to grow their businesses, she realized how much she was learning about color, shapes, accessorizing and putting together a great wardrobe, and she wanted more women to benefit from our wisdom. The result was putting our tips and strategies into this comprehensive book.

Without Caterina's "take action" spirit, her commitment to excellence and her highly-skilled professional publishing team, you would not be reading this book, of which we are all so proud. Our truly dedicated team worked diligently to put together the best possible book for you. We are truly grateful for everyone's stellar contribution.

To Bernie Burson, whose experience in copywriting and copyediting proved invaluable, and whose magic pen and image expertise ensured that this book would be the best it could be.

To LynAnn King, whose positive energy, creativity and image industry savvy provided valuable support, we are truly grateful.

Introduction

"Fashion is general, style is individual; fashion can be bought, style one must possess."
—Edna Woolman Chase, Editor-in-Chief, *Vogue* magazine, 1914-1952

Congratulations! You have opened an incredible resource, packed with great ideas that will guide you to a new vision of yourself. You are about to discover the magic of *My Style, My Way.*

Your personal style is so much more than clothes and fashion. Your style and your image combine to create the message you send out to your friends, family, clients and colleagues every time you walk into a room, a restaurant or an office. In fact, your image is the way you present yourself in all that you say and do! Of course you want your image to be the best it can be—as well as a reflection of your own unique personality and style.

With this book, you can quickly rev up your style, because as top experts in each of our respective specialties, we've joined together to give you the most effective image strategies we know. Some bits of advice are repeated in different chapters—that should tell you how important that advice is!

Each of us has seen how even small changes in your personal image can transform your self-confidence and uplift your spirit. New colors, more flattering styles, a confident carriage and new ways of looking at the world and interacting with others will boost your self-assurance like nothing else. Learning some important travel tips and knowing how to dress and what to shop for during your trip will make your vacation or business trip a memorable one.

It's all here—how-to's for makeup, hair, accessories and foundations, and even how to dress for a date! You'll discover great tips for organizing your closet, building a capsule wardrobe and taking care of those all-important details.

All the image professionals you will meet in this book want you to have the confidence and style to go anywhere and feel and look terrific! We have shared our best tips and proven guidelines to help you reveal your beautiful new style.

To get the most out of this book, we recommend that you read through it once, cover to cover. Then go back and follow the tips that apply to you, in the chapters most relevant to your current situation. Every image improvement you make will make a difference in how you feel and in how others respond to you in your daily personal and professional life.

Developing your personal style can take some time. If you take action and apply the strategies, tips and tactics we share in these pages, you will reap many rewards. With our knowledge and your action, we are confident that, like our thousands of satisfied clients, you too will master the magic of *My Style, My Way.*

To a more stylish new you!

The Co-Authors of *My Style, My Way*

Claiming the Dance of Your Authentic Self
How to Integrate Personal Brand, Image and Civility

By Randa Mufarrij

What would your life be like if you could live every day with purpose, passion and promise? What would be different? How wonder-filled would your life be? This is totally possible for you.

Living from your authentic self is a dance of three parts: personal brand, image and civility. The three together help you create a life of purpose, passion and promise. While each element is important by itself, only when all three are integrated and intertwined can you create meaning and fulfillment in all aspects of your life and in all your relationships. Your authentic self is the foundation for everything good and great!

One of my heroes is Nelson Mandela, president of South Africa. Despite obstacles that would bring many people to their knees, Nelson Mandela never wavered in his desire, his dream. Even when he languished for decades in prison, he went full force toward his goal with love and passion, always with his nation in mind. His confidence and belief in his cause enabled him to face all obstacles and to realize his dream. He became resilient because of this overarching faith and his love for the freedom of others that superseded his self-love.

His efforts have brought him respect, empowerment and awareness. Nelson Mandela is master of his authentic self.

"What lies behind us and what lies before us are tiny matters compared to what lies within us."
—Ralph Waldo Emerson, American poet, lecturer and essayist

Developing and cultivating your authentic self takes effort, time, and dedication; a belief in your ability to make positive changes; a readiness to challenge all obstacles; and a firm commitment to your passion and dream. Is it worth the effort? The answer: a resounding YES!

The Authentic Self Checklist

Answer each question as honestly as you can. Don't think too hard; just choose your initial response.

I am focused on my goals to attain my desired results.	○ *Yes*	○ *Sometimes*	○ *No*
I hold myself accountable for my actions.	○ *Yes*	○ *Sometimes*	○ *No*
I know what my vision and mission are in life, and they are consistent with my life goals.	○ *Yes*	○ *Sometimes*	○ *No*
I am ready for an unexpected change in my career or business.	○ *Yes*	○ *Sometimes*	○ *No*
I am in touch with my passion and it is part of my career or business and life.	○ *Yes*	○ *Sometimes*	○ *No*
I am committed to delivering my authentic brand promise despite all obstacles.	○ *Yes*	○ *Sometimes*	○ *No*

I am so aware of my brand that I constantly carry out my activities and interactions aligned with who I am.	○ *Yes*	○ *Sometimes*	○ *No*
I treat others the way I would like to be treated, with respect and love.	○ *Yes*	○ *Sometimes*	○ *No*
I express my personal social responsibility by giving back to my community.	○ *Yes*	○ *Sometimes*	○ *No*
I am living intentionally, aware of my surroundings and committed to doing things in the right manner so that I am peaceful within myself.	○ *Yes*	○ *Sometimes*	○ *No*

Interpreting your score: Count the number of Yes, Sometimes, and No answers in each column.

Every "yes" on the checklist gives you an overview and some guidelines to assist you in claiming the dance of your authentic self. Once you have completed all the steps and danced to your full potential, you will notice that no matter what challenges you face, you will be determined to live your dream.

Be the Leader of Your Personal Brand

"One man cannot do right in one department of life whilst he is occupied in doing wrong in any other department.
Life is one indivisible whole."
—Mohandas Karamchand Gandhi,
Indian political and spiritual leader

Brands are not created; they are within you. Do you think you have a personal brand? Yes, you do, whether knowingly or unknowingly, implicitly or explicitly. Very simply, it is what people say about you; it is a collection of perceptions—good or bad—that comes from what you do and say and how you act. It is the key to the door of your success and your biggest asset to prosperity. Why is it so important?

- Technology has changed the compass of your direction as an entrepreneur or a career person. No longer do you work in a static organization with job security; this is history. Inventiveness, imagination and differentiation determine success, regardless of where you are in your business or organization.

- Globalization has opened the spheres of competition, and diversity is necessary to differentiate yourself and bring out your uniqueness.

- Within this fast-moving, ever-changing environment, you need to focus, be ready for change, and stay on top of your uniqueness in the workplace and with your target audience.

Personal brand is a tool to help you:

- Consistently clarify and communicate to others who you are, what you stand for, what your direction is and what makes you unique.

- Focus on your goals and achieve your dream.

- Gain confidence, develop presence and create a memorable identity.

- Demonstrate professionalism and authenticity.

- Stay ahead of your competition by differentiating yourself in the marketplace.

Your Personal Brand Starts with Your Vision

In their book, *Career Distinction: Stand Out by Building Your Brand,* published by Wiley in 2007, authors William Arruda and Kirsten

Dixon say, ". . . to build a solid reputation that will catapult you toward your goals, you must understand and be able to articulate what makes you exceptional and compelling." Remember, you are unique.

To find your uniqueness, work with a personal brand strategist and go through the process of finding your vision, purpose and values; clarify your goals, skills, strengths, potential clients and competitors, and fire up your passion to achieve your dream. Get feedback—from the people you know and who know you best—about your brand and what makes you unique. Analyze this feedback and have it professionally evaluated by a personal brand strategist before you integrate it into your brand.

Create a Personal Brand Statement. Once you gather information about your brand, create a "Personal Brand Statement" (PBS) that differentiates you from your competition and captures the essence of your personal brand. Why is the PBS important? It will help you stay focused and on track, will add value to your environment and help you remember to live and breathe your brand. It reminds you of your priorities and is a good tool for communicating your brand to your potential clients—the people you want to reach.

Here is my PBS: *In a leading-edge approach, I motivate globally-minded small business owners to align their personal brand, image, life goals and networks for optimum success.*

Your PBS must make you feel proud. I encourage my clients to read it every day and post it where they can see it. It keeps them on track to align their actions with their decisions to reach their goals.

A volunteer leader at a homeless shelter might have a PBS like this: *I encourage people to serve the needs of those less fortunate, respect the dignity of everyone who asks for help and provide nourishment for both body and soul.*

A writer might have a PBS like this: *Through my writing, I inspire and inform readers to better understand and live their life's purpose.*

> **"Develop a standard for excellence.**
> **Without distinction there is extinction."**
> —Robert Pante, *Dressing to Win*, Doubleday, 1984

Who Do You Know Who Can Communicate Your Brand?

The people closest to you know you best, and when they know your personal brand, they can communicate it on your behalf to the people they know. This widens your brand awareness and your "unique promise of value." How will you communicate your brand to these people? One important way is through networking.

Networking is core to your personal brand. It is how you get your brand message out. Networking has to be fun, not a chore. It is a state of mind and an investment in creating mutually beneficial relationships.

Like any investment, networking needs time, effort, dedication and passion. It is an art that needs to be mastered. However, networking has to be genuine and from the heart. Here are some tips for cultivating connection:

- Stay in touch with your network using online social media and keep them updated on your business.
- Send a snail-mail card, when appropriate, to say thank you, get well, congrats on a new home, graduation, promotion, and so on.
- Send an article that might be of interest, even if you did not write it.
- Ask questions, genuinely listen, live the moment and share.

Monitor what others think of your brand. If their feedback does not support what you want your brand to be, review your actions and words to align them with what you want your brand to be.

Use Your Personal Brand Every Day

You have all the elements you need to tell your story. Now, how will you express your personal brand to become differentiated, unique and prosperous?

Create marketing tools. Start with your biography. This is one of your most important marketing tools since this is where you tell your personal brand story that incorporates what you want your audience to know about you.

Use passion. Make your story compelling, clear, interesting, intriguing, true and unique, so it attracts the people you want to deal with and connects you with them emotionally. This will increase your credibility.

Commit to your personal brand, no matter what communication tool you use. Remember, a strong personal brand is unchanging and always visible to your potential clients. State your key message in all the communication media and choose a mix of media that best reaches your potential clients and with which you feel comfortable. Here are some examples:

- Write professional articles.
- Create a website that represents you clearly.
- Publish a newsletter.
- Volunteer sponsorship for an organization or event that complements your personal brand.

Identify where your potential clients go; what magazines, trade journals and newspapers they read; what organizations they join. Move in the same circles as they do, become an active partner in their success and communicate their personal brand to your brand community. You will start reaping results once you develop the habit of communicating regularly with them, and you will soon attract more like-minded professionals to increase your reach.

> *"You cannot transcend what you do not know;*
> *to go beyond yourself you must know yourself."*
> —Sri Nisargadatta Maharaj, Indian spiritual teacher and philosopher

Be consistent. A unique and strong personal brand always clearly communicates your brand and your "unique promise of value." This attracts people who will contribute to your achieving your goals. You need to be consistent in every communication tool you use. Remember, strong personal brands are constant and visible to potential clients.

Now, move on to the second part of your authentic self—your image.

Be the Leader of Your Image

The more aware you are of your personal brand, the closer you become to the crescendo of the dance of the authentic self. Marrying your brand with your personal image is a crucial step of the dance, and you need to understand what it means so you can achieve your desired goals.

Your image is the impression you send to others. As you may know, people make a judgment about you in the first few seconds they see you. Most of the time, this first impression is also the last impression, and it is difficult to change someone's opinion.

Impression management is one of the most important ways you have of ensuring your image and personal brand complement and support each other. When they are meshed together, you empower your image for optimum impact and greatness. This will put your mind at ease and free it to move toward self-fulfillment and greatness.

Your brand and image come together in three areas: color, clothing and communication. Let's look at each of these components.

Color. Are you skeptical about using color because you do not know much about color harmony? Colors are magical, and specific colors work best with your skin tone and spirit.

Color is one dimension of nonverbal communication. You can relay messages by the colors you wear, and each color portrays different meanings in different cultures.

"Color acts upon the human body; it is the key touched by man to obtain the appropriate vibration from his creative spirit."
—Wassily Kandinsky, Russian artist

You can dress according to your seasonal palette, choosing colors for your personal brand environment according to your personality style and personal attributes. You can use color to express your professional attributes, evoke emotion and build that all-important connection with people who can help your career. Colors you love that do not match your palette can be incorporated in your brand as accent colors. Use color appropriately and consistently.

Clothing. To make a memorable and distinct appearance, put time and effort into choosing clothing. Now that you know what your personal brand is and how you want to portray it, align your clothing with your brand. Look at your long-term goals and dress toward these goals. This is part of being professional and being on top of things. Remember, your appearance is a nonverbal tool that communicates and demonstrates your brand. Your appearance is a reflection of your self-love.

Communication. The way you communicate your personal brand is crucial, and the way you portray your brand has a direct impact on other people's perception of you. Remember, you want your brand to be in the hearts and minds of your potential clients at all times.

Communication is an art, and you need to hone your communication skills so you achieve the best results in any situation. To communicate your brand authentically, you need to be a competent, eloquent communicator and a good listener. If you feel you need to improve in this area, you might consider joining Toastmasters International, an organization that teaches public speaking.

Vocal tone adds a lot to your message. Your voice and words, as well as your style of communication, small talk, ability to start a conversation and so on, are tools for attracting others and making a positive impression. You need to strive for openness, honesty, authenticity, directness and expressiveness in all your verbal and nonverbal communications.

Lead by Example: Civility—The Final Piece of the Authentic Self

"We make a living by what we get. We make a life by what we give."
—Winston Churchill, British orator, author and prime minister

Often, people ask, "Isn't civility the same as etiquette?" Etiquette is one aspect of civility; it is a set of rules about how we conduct ourselves to be socially accepted. Civility is a way of being in the world.

It is important to have good manners, and your personal brand demands it. However, this does not complete the dance of your authentic self. To totally dance the dance, you must walk the walk and talk the talk. Being civil and conducting oneself in a transcending way is always a win-win situation. This is what the authentic self is all about.

Civility is comprised of acts of love toward yourself and others. Loving yourself, loving what you do and loving others are integral to your personal brand and image. When you are kind to others, you learn far more about yourself and you realize what vast pleasure and inner joy come from doing so. When you act with civility, you become empowered, and your inner peace keeps the energy flowing and moving from your inner being to others. This brings your awareness level into a state of truth and enlightenment, and eventually to inner peace and to what we all dream of: world peace. When your personal brand, image and civility work together, you dance the complete dance of your authentic self!

As you can see from the Civility in Action Model™ all things come from a center of civility. It is the foundation of all authentic relationships and is the platform from which you demonstrate your personal brand and image.

> *"Civility is liberating. It frees us from slavery*
> *to self-absorption, impulse and mood."*
> —Dr. P. M. Forni, Professor of Civility and co-founder of
> The Johns Hopkins Civility Project

I coach my clients to use the following principles to set boundaries and allow relationships with others to flourish:

- Treat others with regard, courtesy, kindness and integrity at all times.
- Choose self-control over reaction. Think first, analyze the situation and weigh your actions.
- Aim for win-win solutions.
- Feel a sense of responsibility toward yourself, others and your environment.

Start Now to Create Your Authentic Self

If you want more insights about civility, I encourage you to read *The 25 Rules of Considerate Conduct* by Dr. P.M. Forni, published in 2003 by St. Martin's Griffin.

Start today and reap the rewards of inner peace, enlightenment and truth. When you begin to live from your authentic self, you can move others in the direction of happiness and peace. When other people see how empowering your authentic self is, they are promoted and transported to a higher level of joy and happiness. Happiness is a way of life. It is the art of perceiving ourselves, others and life with transcending delight. With random acts of kindness, politeness and proper social behavior, people become energized, motivated and inspired, and feel the urge to reciprocate with the same kind of actions. They realize that there is still hope on Planet Earth and that happiness is attainable. This comes from being your authentic self!

RANDA MUFARRIJ

*Leading-Edge Image Management for
Globally-Minded Small Business Owners*

**(514) 688-7263
randa@randamufarrij.com
www.randamufarrij.com**

Randa Mufarrij motivates globally-minded business owners to align their personal brand, image, life goals and networks for optimum success. Her international experience and depth of knowledge in personal branding and civility make Randa a certified image consultant with an edge. For over a decade, Randa has worked with professionals in Montreal, Dubai and Lebanon. Her cross-cultural experience in human resources management, event planning, fashion and aesthetics have sharpened her understanding of beauty and human development and helped her connect with clients.

Randa uses an integrated approach that centers on personal responsibility. As a Reach-Certified Personal Branding Strategist, Randa is among the first image consultants trained to guide entrepreneurs in the discovery of their unique value in order to develop their authentic, memorable style. In her Civility in Action™ programs, participants achieve the best outcomes through genuine respect and communication.

Randa is a leader of the Civility Project committee and the Ambassadors Program for the Association of Image Consultants International, and is the recipient of the 2010 AICI Civility Star Award. She is an active member of Toastmasters International and has obtained certifications in neurolinguistic programming and human resources management from McGill University.

Radiance—The Finishing Touch

By Monica Brandner

In 1998, I was privileged to represent the magnificent state of Alaska in the Mrs. United States Pageant. Many would consider my experience a Cinderella fairy tale and in some ways, this is true. However, I compare my story more to Sleeping Beauty, for I was asleep in certain areas of my life before this experience. Transformation and an "ultimate makeover" were part of the preparation I underwent for my spectacular, red-carpet event.

As a pageant queen, part of my training included learning to be radiant. Investing in this area of my life has paid big dividends and was well worth the effort. It has been about finding the balance between authentic beauty—what I wear on the outside, and authentic grace—that with which I "wardrobe" my heart. I am a walking billboard. What I do and say, and what I wear, all tell the story of me. Likewise, what you do and say and wear tell the story of you.

We often compliment women on their shoes. I have a pair of black Stuart Weitzman's, with rhinestones up the back, that turns heads. However, what really catches a person's eye is a woman who walks tall and confident.

Radiance can take an ordinary woman and make her extraordinary. I believe your desire is to look better, feel better and create a winning image. Consider this chapter as life lessons from a pageant queen. My intention here is to inspire you to take action to experience illumination in your style, your way.

Crowns made of gems sparkle! What follows is a chapter of "gems." When you find your true, unique beauty—inside and out, and adorn yourself with grace, you will be highly sought after.

Let's get started!

A Queen Has a Positive Outlook

"If you want your life to be more rewarding, you have to change the way you think."
—Oprah Winfrey,
American television host, producer and philanthropist

Why do so many women struggle with issues of self-image and worthlessness? The view you have of yourself will direct your life! When I decided to run for Mrs. Alaska, my self-perception was distorted. My mirror spoke: "You're inadequate, . . . you don't measure up, . . . you don't have the perfect body." In other words, I thought I wasn't good enough. Okay—stop! To whom was I comparing myself? Possibly to images from:

• Hollywood

• Magazines

• Television

• Friends

What do *you* want out of life? Insecurity and inferiority can extinguish your dreams and steal opportunities and abilities to believe in yourself.

When inferiority speaks, looking in the mirror can be painful. As we listen to inferiority's voice, we focus on how imperfect our bodies are and how ugly we think we look. It takes tenacity to overcome these toxic emotions. Let's hear from one such tenacious woman:

"How I see or value myself fluctuates like the stock market. I was selling myself short. Now, I set my own value. It is what I say it is! Self-value should not be defined by magazines, movies or what others think, but by what I think and know in my own heart to be true. I am not defined by my looks, accomplishments or failures. I am defined by my choices. When I get knocked down, I get back up, recover and try again. When I changed my outlook, I started liking who I am. I now have healthier relationships, and opportunities have opened up for me professionally. The mirror doesn't define who I am anymore. I do! I stopped listening to its deceptive lies."

Guard your thought life so it won't shake your confidence. This is our challenge—to let go of the negative and think about those things in your life that are lovely. When you have a bad hair day, focus on your assets. Yes, you *do* have assets! Think: which of your features elicit compliments from your friends?

- Hair
- Eyes
- Complexion
- Teeth

- Waist
- Legs
- Ankles
- Lips *(lipstick is a woman's main accessory)*

Self-acceptance can be a struggle. But when you are at peace with your body, it will begin to show. One key to looking fabulous is to dress according to your body type or to camouflage problem areas. Here are some ways to do just that!

1. A jacket is a wardrobe star. It adds instant polish and hides problem areas with ease.

2. If you have a thick waist and want to create an illusion of looking thinner, wear a tunic top.

3. Are you bigger on top? Wear a scoop or V neckline.

Remember, we all have things we don't love about our bodies. The good news is we don't have to live life naked! For more on dressing for your body type, see Johonna Duckworth's chapter, *Be True to Your Shape,* on page 61.

Relax. Look for clothes that fit your body type and make you feel amazing. Purchase only those items you absolutely love. Remember, self-acceptance will make you shine brighter.

Gems:

• Every woman has something she does not like about her body.

• You were born with a certain body type, coded into your DNA.

• Your body is unique. You are not a cookie cutter of someone else.

• Don't let society or culture dictate how you should dress, walk, talk, look or act.

• Take care of your clothing. Use wooden hangers, steam the wrinkles out and sew on buttons that fall off. Note—Nordstrom® will sew on your buttons free if you've purchased your clothing in their store.

Now, smile! Look in the mirror and say, "It's a new day, so . . . hello, Gorgeous!"

A Queen Radiates Vitality

Depression, worry, anxiety and anger never look good on anyone. When our hearts are broken and full of negative emotions, we lose our ability to shine.

Life happens and sometimes, "It is what it is." According to the American Institute of Stress, 75 to 90 percent of all visits to primary care physicians are for stress-related problems. Stress extinguishes the luminescence in our life.

Although we may try, we cannot change others, or even our own circumstances at times. We can only change ourselves. Take responsibility for yourself only. Don't try to change other people. Say, "I am tired of my old life! Today I am going to change my attitude, my approach, how I treat others, and my thought-life."

Gems:

- Pick up the book, *The Happiness Project,* by Gretchen Rubin, published in 2009 by Harper, or *The Creation Health Breakthrough* by Monica Reed, MD, published in 2007 by Center Street.

- Ask yourself, "What would make me happier—a cleaner closet, less yelling, a closer relationship with my spouse?" Now do something about it.

- Laughter is good medicine. Lighten up!

- Seek out a counselor, spiritual leader or life coach if you need help.

- Always remember—new beginnings are available at any moment, 365 days a year, and it's never too late to begin again.

Toxic emotions kill, steal and destroy relationships and your happiness. Without happiness, you will not experience radiant living. Activating forgiveness, love, joy and peace will bring vitality to your life.

A Queen Plans what She Needs

Taking care of ourselves—body, soul and mind—is key to becoming radiant. Do you want to stand out in a crowd and go from worn-out to WOW? Embrace these winning combinations if you wish to look luminous.

Drink Water. Try adding lemon, sliced strawberries and a green tea bag. The tea and water combined create a natural power boost. Anti-aging is another benefit.

Exercise. I build stamina by incorporating walking, Pilates® or a "boot camp" style workout into my day. Stretching gives me an instant boost of energy. Using a personal trainer changed my life. Don't be intimidated. Your trainer may become your best friend.

Nutrition. Shop at farmers' markets. When in a grocery store, shop the perimeter and stay away from pre-made and packaged foods. Eat fruits, vegetables, fish and nuts, and don't forget milk. There are some great recipes in Prevention® magazine. Healthy eating should be a lifestyle, not a diet! And every once in a while, a girl has to have her chocolate, so I indulge. It puts a smile on my face.

Sleep. When I'm tired and worn out, it shows. Get seven to nine hours of sleep a night. Sleep helps us stay sharp, focused and energized all day. Sleep also helps us heal from the demands of the previous day.

Rest. Ever feel like you want to run away from life? Burnout is real. Take time to get away, whether it's in your back yard, lying on a hammock, taking a nap, watching snowflakes fall as you drink something warm by the fire, floating down a river on an inner tube with the sun kissing your face or checking into a hotel with a day spa. I call it "rejuvenation therapy" and it will definitely look good on you!

Prayer/meditation. I am passionate about prayer. Prayer is a great release for me. When something concerns me, I pray about it. I see it as a call for help—my petition. Prayer is a great remedy for worry and anxiety. When I meditate, I think of what is true, noble, reputable, authentic, compelling, gracious, the best (not the worst), the beautiful (not the ugly), whatever is admirable—anything excellent. Remember to count your blessings. Gratitude is transforming. Studies show that thankfulness is a key to happiness. When self-confidence exudes from a joyful person, she is dazzling! Try prayer or meditation or some form of quiet reflection, focusing on gratitude. You will love the results.

A Queen Is Never Dressed without Her Smile

One way to stand out in a crowd is to smile. A smile is magnetic. Don't be afraid to use tooth-whitener if needed. A fresh smile is an accessory you don't want to leave home without.

Gems:
Benefits of a smile:

- Smiling makes you look younger.

- A smile improves your health and stress level.

- Your smile is welcoming and makes others feel they are worth your attention.

- Smiling is the trademark of a happy, positive person.

- Smiling people appear more confident, are more likely to be promoted and are more likely to be approached.

- Radiant women can change a moment with a smile!

When a Queen Rushes, She Falls

There is something to be said about having good posture in high heels. I learned to carry myself with confidence, turn on the balls of my feet, walk slowly and elegantly glide across the floor. My walk had purpose.

If I'm in a hurry, I seem out of control and can easily trip or fall. I practice walking slowly so I don't lose my composure. My appearance is my introduction to the world; it tells everyone who I am. Feeling at ease shows I am controlled and polished.

Gems:
Relaxing tips

- Sit in the sun and close your eyes (of course, put on your 30 protection sunscreen first) and drink something cold.

- Take a friend to coffee, tea, lunch or dinner.

- Listen to soft music and light a candle.

- Bake cupcakes and be creative with your decorations. My daughter does this to relax. She is like the "Ace of Cupcakes."

- Take your daughter or granddaughter to high tea. Plant some time and love into the next generation. If you do not have children, tea with your girlfriends can be exquisite.

- Hang out in a garden or visit nature.

Remember, if you fall it's never too late to get back up again. Do something nice for yourself, and don't forget to put your feet up and relax every once in awhile.

A Queen Walks in Authentic Grace

The votes for Mrs. Congeniality came in and they called my name. I was shocked! "Me?" I thought. "Wow! What an honor." The dictionary defines congeniality as "a pleasant disposition; friendly and sociable." Being congenial causes others to notice and want to be around you. Kindness and respect are always a winning combination.

I love this quote from my mentor, Deborah King, of Final Touch Finishing School, Inc.: "Civility—Always in style—Wardrobe basic—Perfect accessory—Fits everybody!"

Grace is civility—a very attractive quality because it showcases itself in the form of beautiful actions, words or deeds. Having *authentic* grace can pay dividends in your relationships, both personal and professional.

We each have a reputation. Rude behavior is never stylish or attractive. If I asked people about your style of behavior, how would they describe you?

- Kind
- Patient
- Loving

- Considerate
- Giving
- Encouraging

Avoid being gossipy, judgmental, angry, jealous, a backstabber, prideful or bitter. Our behavior impacts others. It draws people *to* us or pushes them *away*. We don't always realize that what we say and do affects others.

Gems:

- If you struggle with rude behavior or low self-worth, seek some professional help from a counselor, spiritual leader, or life or etiquette coach. There is nothing wrong with realizing that sometimes we need help.
- Our words and actions bring life or death, light or darkness to others and ourselves.
- A kind word refreshes like a spring shower.
- None of us have arrived. We all have room for improvement.

Ladies, change requires change, and that first step to change is to wake up! The progression looks like this: Wake up, stand up, get ready and walk out the door. When you have an "Aha!" moment, make a decision, study and practice—then transformation comes.

Becoming radiant takes work. But remember, for a diamond to be brilliant it must be polished. When the process is finished, it is valuable.

Find a mentor. This book is a great resource of North America's top image and etiquette experts who care about you.

Our goal: We want *you* to shine and be crowned with success!

Remember, a woman who finds her true, unique beauty and adorns herself with grace is a woman highly sought after. Her self-worth and confidence is attractive. Her value is compared to rubies. She has the power to turn ordinary moments to extraordinary ones by:

- The way she dresses
- The words she speaks
- Her gestures
- Her acts of kindness

Now, arise, shine and watch the room light up when you walk in!

MONICA BRANDNER
IMAGE by m. brandner

*Etiquette and image can open doors,
but integrity keeps them open*

(509) 688-5892
monica@imagebymonica.com
www.imagebymonica.com

Monica is president of an image and etiquette business located in Juneau, Alaska, and Spokane, Washington. She is certified through Final Touch Finishing School and is a member of the Association of Image Consultants International and Toastmasters International.

As Mrs. Alaska 1998, Monica spent her year speaking to and encouraging women and youth to recognize their value and worth. Wearing pageant shoes taught her life is full of opportunities and being prepared is crucial to one's success. Whether it's a job interview, promotion, potential business client or a pageant, doors can open or close based on messages we send in our dress and behavior. The combination of a polished image and strong social skills is important for prosperity in today's global society.

Along with owning her own business, Monica works for Alaska/ Horizon Airlines and provides professional etiquette training to their customer service team. She is also a source of expertise for radio, television, newspaper and magazine articles. Monica has a heart for the next generation of women and volunteers her time organizing events for teen girls, ages 12–18, called "Radiant."

Signature Image from the Heart
Cultivate Yours from the Inside Out

By Jeanne Patterson, RN, MBA

"Each of us has that right, that possibility, to invent ourselves daily. If a person does not invent herself, she will be invented. So, to be bodacious enough to invent ourselves is wise."
—Maya Angelou, American poet laureate and author

What good is it to look fantastic if you do not feel fantastic? What is the point of others admiring your beauty if you feel ugly? There is no value in creating your personal style if you do not first cultivate self-esteem. True personal style comes from each of us realizing that we are unique, beautiful and wonderful, and always a work in progress. As you enter each stage of life, there are new adventures to enjoy and challenges to overcome. Your physical appearance, emotional development, and spiritual ideals change throughout life's journey.

Your personal style is partially made up of your body image: the picture you have of your physical appearance in your mind. The way you feel about your body can have a big impact on how you feel about yourself as a whole. We can receive many conflicting messages from family, the media and our culture about what is considered ideal. Unrealistic or unhealthy messages can negatively impact your self–concept if you let them. Instead, you can conceptualize your own sense of great style by focusing on your unique mental, physical and spiritual qualities. Male and female bodies are special in their own ways. Focus on your strengths and become a lifelong learner to continually improve. Confidence looks good on everyone and vibrant energy attracts positive people!

Self-esteem is how you feel about yourself as a person. You can cultivate a positive self-image and minimize your negative perceptions. You can craft good self-esteem by practicing self-care and establishing optimal health as your foundation.

During my early career as a critical care nurse, my experience strengthened an acute awareness of people as holistic beings. Alterations in our environment—including temperature, light, nutrient intake, noise level, tactile sensation, humidity and smell—are key factors in human wellness and function. Our body systems are highly interactive. They are designed to sustain wellness.

Your lifestyle drives the care of your body, mind and spirit. A nutritious diet that fosters optimal vitality will generate true beauty. Sleep is also key for beauty and good health. Frequent travel disrupts your sleep patterns and your circadian rhythms. Adequate sleep promotes cell renewal and stabilizes moods. An escape to a quiet environment encourages meditative states and spiritual peace.

"Every time you smile at someone, it is an action of love,
a gift to that person, a beautiful thing."
—Mother Teresa of Calcutta,
Catholic nun and Nobel Peace Prize recipient

Nourish Your Body and Spirit

Another aspect of cultivating your personal style is promoting inner peace and contentment by accepting who you are. You can improve your life by eating less processed food. If certain foods do not agree with your body I recommend you seek a medical evaluation for food allergies. Ensure you have appropriate and adequate vitamin intake to sustain optimal body function. Search for locally grown organic food. As more people buy organic food from local farms, the prices decrease. Below are some health maintenance tips to improve your beauty from the inside out:

- Eat enough fiber to sustain effective movement of nutrients through the body.

- Decrease the high-sugar foods in your diet such as pastries and candies.

- Eliminate sugar-filled sodas and drink more water.

- Integrate cardiovascular, strength-training and stretching exercises into your daily lifestyle.

- Meditate or take time for quiet reflection daily.

- Ensure adequate sleep (7-8 hours) to minimize crankiness and appetite spikes.

- Make your healthy smile a priority with regular, excellent dental care. This is very important, not just for looks, but also for heart health.

- Limit excessive sun exposure and use sunscreen with SPF 20 or higher.

I have worked with clients from their twenties into their fifties. Whatever your chronological age, you can look and feel great. Phenomenal advances in medicine over the past 30 years allow us to enjoy being active throughout our life. Human life spans are increasing toward age 90. I know you want to remain active, be mentally alert, look good and feel comfortable for your whole life.

I invite you to do the following exercise on a day you have set aside for self-care, on a day you are feeling relaxed.

1. Set aside some time to look in the mirror.

2. As you look at your reflection, think of yourself with loving kindness.

3. Notice your unique gifts—for example, kindness, intelligence, courage.

4. List your positive physical attributes—perhaps thick, wavy hair, creamy skin, a strong back, intense eyes, shapely legs, embraceable curves!

5. Smile to improve your facial expression.

6. Smile to support positive emotions such as joy and happiness.

7. Minimize any negative concepts and thoughts.

8. Emphasize the positive—for example, twinkling blue eyes; soft, sensitive brown eyes; mysterious blue or green eyes.

9. Give thanks for your marvelous, miraculous machine—the human body.

Self-care is always a good idea. This is an exercise you can do often to remind you of how wonderful you and your body are. If you are having a low self-esteem day, this can help snap you out of it.

Make Room for More Kindness

In addition to this exercise, discover more ways to be kind to yourself. Reward yourself in small, tangible ways for your beauty, your heart and your large and small accomplishments. Treat yourself to a manicure, a relaxing body massage, a great hairstyle or a flowing silk scarf in a favorite color. Know that all actions provide learning experiences and look upon any "mistakes" as valuable learning and development opportunities!

Outside influences can be hard on us from childhood to adulthood. It can be difficult to sustain positive self-love in this environment. Make your self-care and self love a priority. If you take the time to nurture yourself in small ways, it will make a big difference.

> *"I can be changed by what happens to me.*
> *But I refuse to be reduced by it."*
> —Maya Angelou, American poet laureate and author

As you focus on the positive aspects of your life and self-development, you may find you smile more. A smile is your most important fashion accessory. You can hear a smile in someone's voice. People feel welcomed by a handshake and a smile.

Acknowledge Life Transitions

Life demands change along its exciting journey. We will face many transitions as the years pass. Our bodies will transition as well. Consider the following questions when an inevitable transition occurs:

- Do you want to celebrate a new look for a new body?

- Are you ready to change or upgrade your appearance to prepare for or support you through a life transition?

- Do you have the desire to dress to impress for a special occasion?

- Have you faced medical challenges that have altered your body's shape?

- Are you ready to dive back into the dating pool?

Consider working with an image consultant to help navigate the changes life brings to everyone. An image consultant can bring professional perspective and input. He or she should work in partnership with you to develop solutions tailored to your personal needs.

People in their forties and beyond often face major life transitions such as the loss of a spouse through death or divorce, career changes and children leaving the nest. Major weight gain or loss can alter body proportions. These events may stimulate a need to reinvent your image. Your image consultant can help you achieve your new goals.

Know the Effects of Color on Mind and Culture

"The chief function of color should be to serve expression."
—Henri Matisse, French painter and sculptor

Color has a strong impact on human beings. Have you ever noticed how a color will imprint itself on your mind or carry a specific message? Nature presents colors that may indicate restfulness or danger. The combination of yellow and black stripes may provoke a feeling of danger because some stinging insects have this pattern. Poisonous snakes may have bright yellow, orange and black in striped or zigzag patterns—another danger alert.

You easily notice different shades and hues of color. The green shades of grass and forest can be calming. The clear azure blue of a summer sky can be uplifting to the spirit. The transparent turquoise waters found in tropical environments may stimulate curiosity and tranquility.

In her book, *Color Healing,* published by DK Publishing in 2001, Stephanie Norris discusses how personal color can influence you. Since ancient civilization, people have used color in healing practices. Color can have a psychological impact on human beings. You can experiment with color by noting which colors appeal to you. When you try on an appealing color, how does it make you feel?

Red excites the senses. Courage, passion and blood are associated with red. Blue exemplifies loyalty and calmness in corporate culture. Yellow often brightens the mood and stimulates thinking. Black carries an air of authority and can be somber. Purple results from the combination of blue and red. It has been associated with royalty and meditative states. Green will often calm people. Much of the natural world contains shades of green. White may symbolize purity.

One example of color symbolism is seen in the U.S. flag. From the book *Our Flag,* published in 1989 by the House of Representatives:

"The colors of the pales (the vertical stripes) are those used in the flag of the United States of America; White signifies purity and innocence, Red, hardiness & valour, and Blue, the color of the Chief (the broad band above the stripes) signifies vigilance, perseverance & justice."
—Charles Thompson, Secretary of the Continental Congress

Note that colors with a particular symbolic meaning in one culture can carry a different meaning in another culture. Some colors develop a specific symbolism related to political history, religious observances or ethnic background.

Below are some intriguing color essentials.

Red. In China, red means good luck and celebration. In India, it means purity. However, in South Africa, red symbolizes mourning. People in Western cultures associate red with danger, love, passion and excitement.

Yellow. Yellow symbolizes courage in Japan. In Egypt, it means mourning. Western culture associates yellow with hazard and hope.

Blue. Blue symbolizes defeat and trouble to Cherokees. In Iran, blue means heaven and spirituality. In Western societies, it means conservative and corporate, and can also describe depression and sadness.

Orange. This color indicates creativity. It is associated with Halloween in the West. It is also linked with Protestants in Ireland.

Purple. In Thailand, purple is the color of mourning for widows, while in Western culture it symbolizes royalty and spirituality.

Green. The color green is affiliated with Islam in India. It is widely known as the symbol for the entire country of Ireland and thus for Saint Patrick's Day. People in Western culture equate this color with spring, rebirth or renewal.

White. In Japan, white carnations symbolize mortality. Eastern culture connects this color with funerals. Western culture associates white with brides, angels, good guys' hats, hospitals, nurses, doctors and peace—the white dove.

Black. In China, the color for young boys is black. In Western cultures, black is tied to funerals, death, and—when combined with orange, evildoers and rebellion—Halloween.

Color inspires, excites and affects visual design perception. It adds vibrancy to life. Your reaction to color can be both physical and emotional. When choosing colors for your wardrobe, think about how you want to feel and which colors will enhance that feeling.

A personal color evaluation by an image consultant can reveal your most flattering colors. These are the colors that will make your presence pop! From these, you may choose specific colors to represent your most important brand—you. Do you want to look fabulous? Color can be part of your "wow" factor. For more about personal color, see Dawn Stebbing's chapter, *Enhance Your Image with Color,* on page 49.

Your Personal Style

The phrase "my style, my way" carries a special meaning for me. It means the courage and aesthetic sense to execute your own style strategy. Keep in mind your personal values.

- Do you want to appear soft and romantic?
- Do you love the sensuous feel of silk on freshly-showered skin?
- Are you sports-minded and do you love classic, uncluttered lines?
- Are you sultry, yet needing to maintain modesty?
- Do you emphasize a low-key, natural and low-maintenance lifestyle?
- Is your career position one which is conservative and carries authority?
- Do cultural norms influence your style of dress?

You can establish self-determined personal aesthetic goals. You can differentiate yourself through selection of artistic, symbolic touches which capitalize on your color, ethnic pride or sentimental affiliations. Jewelry, fabric patterns and accessories sometimes carry symbolic meanings.

Perhaps a beloved grandparent passed down a treasured brooch, watch or earrings. Each time you wear this piece, you may remember guiding principles, humorous stories or the person's loving kindness. An antique locket could hold a lock of hair or family pictures. Sentimental objects can be especially dear.

People across all ages and cultures have a thirst for life and the desire to put their best foot forward. Your exposure to global cultures facilitates better understanding. Greater knowledge paves the way toward improved personal and business relationships. As the world becomes a smaller place, unique cultural values and practices can be acknowledged.

Be a lifelong learner. Cross-cultural and global knowledge add to your appeal and make you a more well-rounded individual. Take the initiative and time to learn about different cultural values and practices. The hardest words to say can be "I'm sorry." In a different cultural context, your actions can carry unintended meanings.

> *"A little consideration, a little thought for others,*
> *makes all the difference."*
> —Winnie-the-Pooh, via A. A. Milne, English author

Our new era of social networks remains an exploration of human connection. The line between acceptable inquiry and connection continues to evolve. The speed of life seems to accelerate with our technology. We strive to remember and honor the mind/body/spirit needs for adequate pacing, rejuvenation and privacy. Immediate access to world events affects almost everyone.

Learned humility and consideration for others forms the basis of social etiquette and smooth interpersonal relationships. Active listening, quiet observation and intuitive problem solving may be the most difficult practices to incorporate into your personal interactions. Body language and cultural awareness require study and sensitivity.

When you develop your individual style, etiquette could be the intangible asset which makes you stand out. I think Maya Angelou's memorable quote says it best:

> *"I've learned that people will forget what you said,*
> *people will forget what you did,*
> *but people will never forget how you made them feel."*
> —Maya Angelou, American poet laureate and author

Your complete image and personal style encompass many elements. Remember to include self-esteem, self-care and an increased awareness of life's transitions. Consider the impact of color as those aspects which touch hearts and minds and make you and your style even more extraordinary!

JEANNE PATTERSON, RN, MBA
Pattern Signature Image

Caring, Educating, Transforming

(503) 550-0051
jp@pattersonsignatureimage.com
www.pattersonsignatureimage.com

Jeanne is a New England native. New Englanders are known for their dedicated work ethic, pride in quality workmanship and eye for economic value. An acute intellect, common sense, artistic flair, and a natural holistic health viewpoint have served her well during extensive travel for business and pleasure.

Her parents passed on hard-won lessons acquired from the Great Depression. Her mother taught her about quality clothing construction during shopping excursions to upscale thrift shops as a child. Her father was a hair stylist and an active member of the local community. Changing fashions, economic trends and world affairs were family conversation topics.

As a lifelong health care advocate, Jeanne brings a gentle sense of humor, patience, quick wit and genuine caring to relationships. These traits foster effective mentorship and conflict resolution capabilities. Friends have described her as smart, creative, tenacious, detail-oriented, highly intuitive and approachable. Jeanne's volunteer activities include: Dress for Success®, Toastmasters International and the Association of Image Consultants International. She now resides in Portland, Oregon.

Dressing Your Personality Style

By Kim Mittelstadt

Take a moment and visualize something you loved from your childhood. We all have a memory of one special thing: A favorite stuffed animal, a soft blankie with ragged ends or perhaps a beautiful pink dress adorned with lace. Remember the sense of comfort you associated with this object or the special pride when you wore that dress? Why do you think you felt so good? Was it the shape, the texture, the colors, the smell? It could have been a combination of these. Such good feelings culminate in one thing: positive energy.

There were no outside influences causing these feelings at this age; they were absolutely pure emotions. In today's world, a myriad of outside influences affect every aspect of our lives, including the way we view ourselves and even the clothes we wear. Positive energy comes from understanding our personality. Choosing an outfit and just simply getting dressed for the day is one of the most important events of our day and an integral element in determining how we are going to feel. Let's discover how you can reintroduce these pure emotions into your lives; to surround yourself with positive energy, which leads to your authentic self and ultimately to an understanding of your personality style.

Personality and Self Discovery

There are several factors in determining your personality traits that will lead you to your personality style. A few of the main factors are your skin tone (coloring), bone structure and your natural–born behaviors. You are born into this world with a predetermined personality unique to you. However, family, environment, and even something as seemingly insignificant as your birth order, may have influenced you to behave in ways opposite to your intrinsic behaviors or personal style. So the most critical question is, how do you determine who you were born into this world to be, and how do you attain your perfect harmonious style? We are going to explore ways to know how to wear your clothes with confidence and pride, and not have your clothes wear you!

I have had the privilege of working with many uniquely talented individuals who were so confused with attempting to identify their own personal style that they were unable to communicate effectively with others. Many could no longer pinpoint what truly made them happy. But through the process of self–discovery, they were able to transform themselves into people who now enjoy all the excitement of personally fulfilling lives.

At points in your adolescence, you may have experienced outside pressures that greatly influenced your actions, creating "safety boundaries" that may or may not have been to your advantage. However, once you became a young adult, you assumed control of your life and were ready to greet the world!

Unlocking Your Personal Style

Through trial and error, you have explored clothing styles, behaviors and communication styles that may have left your observers with

with mixed signals. Try changing your clothing style by adding a little personal flair, cautiously at first, so as not to step too far into unfamiliar style territory. As an example, I was always told by my mother that I should not wear black. I was later color analyzed as a "winter" at the world-renowned Fashion Academy, in the '80s when the four seasons color concept was popular. My instructor suggested I take the blond highlights out of my hair and go back to my true brunette color. I did so, and I was able to wear black—very successfully! I finally gave myself permission to create my own identity and accept my uniqueness. My personal transformation had begun. I was discovering my personal style.

Communication Styles

Understanding and embracing all personality styles will help you appreciate others as well as give you the ability to communicate more effectively. The lack of understanding of personality types may be the very cause of many of our miscommunications. Have you ever noticed the differences in newborns when you play with them? Some babies respond and play, often for hours, while others play for only short periods with short attention spans. You are born into the world with introverted or extroverted behaviors. Your primary personality type defines who you are, while your secondary style is the means by which you express your primary style. By understanding these different styles, you will reach a level of confidence in communicating that will give you a positive advantage over someone who has not studied this form of communication. Your comfort level with yourself and how you feel from the inside out will manifest itself through your positive energy and will magnetically attract others.

As you explore this concept, you will surpass the infamous first impression scenario and be pleasantly surprised at how people will listen to and trust you more than ever before. Not dressing in harmony with your personality type or wearing the wrong style or colors may create confusion to your observers, distracting them from what you are really trying to communicate. In today's highly-competitive world, this could be devastating.

Understanding How to Define Your Personality Style

Think of style as a glass of milk. Let's say you were to add a drop of chocolate to your milk. The color may not change; however, the flavor now has a hint of chocolate taste. Now add a few more drops of chocolate. Not only has the color changed because the milk has more chocolate influence, but it also tastes sweeter. This is how our clothing styles, personalities, mannerisms and overall behavior differ, which is what makes us unique. If you were to take your personal "glass of milk" and add environment, upbringing, family influence and even your birth order, you are now that unique "one of a kind."

Body Types and Personality Style

Our body types also play a key role in determining our personal style. There are very few people who have perfectly-proportioned figures. Not only will different characteristics determine what style of clothing we will ultimately be most comfortable wearing, there are also general characteristics in women's body types that lead them to gravitate toward certain styles. If you are inclined to use fashion magazines and the media to help you choose styles, I recommend bookmarking a few of the styles that you find appealing. At a later date, go back through them and ask yourself, "What was it about this garment that most attracted me? Was it the color, the pattern, the overall shape of the garment?" Your body type and bone structure will influence your best choice of fabrics, patterns, colors and accessories when creating overall balance in your appearance.

There are unlimited shapes and sizes of women all wanting the same thing—to feel attractive and authentic. You must determine what is attractive and authentic for you. Participating in a style analysis will train you to use illusion dressing to create your perfect style. For example, by dressing in all one color or in a pattern with a vertical influence, you will create the illusion of being taller and thinner. Fabric textures also need to be taken into consideration when choosing clothing styles. Although patterns have the power to add interest to your outfits, keep in mind if the fabric is too light or heavy or the pattern is too big or small, it can project a negative impression if worn by the wrong body type. If you have a petite frame, large patterns and stiff, heavy fabrics are overpowering and you may get lost in your garment. If you have a fuller figure, it is best to wear lighter-weight fabrics to keep yourself balanced proportionally.

Once we are attracted to a specific garment, our natural inclination is to reach out and feel the fabric. Have you ever tried to exchange a baby's "blankie" for something else? My twin boys would not in a million years settle for the other one's blanket. We even create texture preferences at an early age.

Color and Style Personality

Color is energy. Choosing your perfect color palette is a vital component in creating your style. The primary determinant when choosing your best colors is your skin tone. Color, when worn correctly, creates moods for the wearer and viewer alike. It can be calming or stimulating. Wearing the correct color will give you positive energy and is the very first thing that people notice. Choosing the correct contrast levels based on the relative lightness and darkness (value) of your skin tone, eyes and hair will create overall harmony in your style. Generally speaking, if your features are lighter and softer, medium- to lower-contrast levels of the same or similar colors, or color values, will work best to create overall balance and harmony. The more contrast in your skin, hair and eyes, the easier it is to wear high-contrast color combinations such as black and white or cream and navy.

Keep in mind, energy is the key. Before you impulsively buy another item of clothing or accessory that will join other orphans in your wardrobe, I recommend you have a personality assessment, color analysis and style consultation performed by a professional image consultant. This will save you both time and money, and you will love creating your new wardrobe, knowing exactly who you are and why you are attracted to certain items. Take time to really explore your feelings and energy level each time you shop.

Determining Your Personality Style

There are four main personality styles that are directly related to the colors of your skin, eyes and hair. By understanding how to best apply these qualities to your wardrobe every day, you will develop strategies to accentuate your positive features and overcome your style challenges, reaching your full style potential.

Most of us can relate to something in each of the categories described below, which will give you a clearer picture of the different style types. Keep in mind, you will favor your most prominent style and be influenced in differing degrees by the other three style types, creating your overall unique personality style. As you embark on your quest of style discovery, embrace these differences and enjoy personalizing your own style.

Read through the descriptions below, relate each description to yourself and for each, try to determine if you feel energetic or if you feel pulled down. Number them one to four (one for the most energy, four for the least), then go back to the styles in the magazines you bookmarked earlier. Do these styles fall into your numbering pattern? If yes, then you are on the road to creating your personal style. If no, identify what it is about the garment or outfit that attracted you. Is it the color, fabric or style? Will it complement your body type and coloring? Now visualize yourself in the garment. How does it make you feel? Energetic? Attractive? Don't be afraid to critique your clothing choices to justify your selections. Eventually, you will be able to accomplish this task on a subconscious level. Be prepared to save time, money and energy. Take note of your findings and keep going—you are on your way.

Dramatic personalities leave their viewers with a feeling of admiration. You are an eye-catching, stunning, well-put-together individual. With your natural—yet glamorous and striking—look, your gorgeous appearance is highlighted with medium- to high-contrast color combinations in solid colors or bold prints. You enjoy challenges and are self-motivated and goal-driven. A meticulously fashionable hairstyle suits you well as long as it makes a statement. Your favorite colors are bold, just like your personality. Take care when wearing black; it is your power color and may make you seem intimidating to other personality styles. You are savvy at accessorizing with flair and look radiant when you're dressed in total harmony.

Natural personalities have a simple, uncomplicated appearance. You are attracted to earth-toned colors and love garments that are relaxed, with flat, smooth textures and easy-to-care-for fabrics. You look great in muted yet rich warm tones and prefer no-fuss hairstyles and little to no makeup. As a natural, you aren't big on too many accessories; you prefer comfort and practicality in your style, medium to low heels and natural materials. With your informal personality, you are easily approachable. However, take care not to dress too casually in a business atmosphere. Of all the personality styles, Naturals are known as the peacemakers of life.

Classic personalities are feminine and soft in appearance. With your self-disciplined personality style, you are organized and detail-oriented. You are most comfortable in soft and flowing fabrics accented with small, delicate patterns, lace or bows. You have fresh, feminine qualities that are attractive to men. Because there is usually medium contrast between your hair and skin tone, colors of medium value are most flattering. Hairstyles for the romantic are soft and feminine. You will find them in all lengths, as long as there is lots of volume.

Artistic personalities are innovative, full of life, and creative with their style choices. You are inspiring and carefree and look best in bright, clear colors with high contrast to match your outgoing personality. Your philosophy behind choosing accessories is "anything goes." With your lively, creative qualities, you become an original of your own style. Free-spirited and edgy, you love experimenting with makeup colors and colorful hair streaks; if it makes a statement, you own it!

Now take that same energy level from the description that excited you the most (the one you chose as number one—most energy) and transfer those feelings to your wardrobe. Use your internal energy thermometer to begin your adventure. Have a personal fashion show with yourself and try on all your favorite pieces first. Your goal is to re-create the positive energy with those preferred garments. Once you have completed this task, chart your clothing pieces on a piece of paper categorized by tops, bottoms, jackets and color. Now, move on to the orphans that have been hanging in your closet. You have created feelings that you need to transfer to each piece of clothing. Look at the color, style and length of your accessories and garments and see what gives you energy. If something doesn't seem right, try to determine what it is and change it or get rid of it.

It's time for you to create your own "wow factor." By expressing positive energy with your clothing style and behavior, you will create a captivating style that radiates a totally positive image. By systematically choosing your style and colors, you will be at a distinct advantage over others who have not been trained and do not understand the value of discovering how to incorporate personality into their personal style. You will be comfortable and happy with the style you have created for yourself. I want you to have confidence inside and out, head to soul. When you try on clothing, accessories, or even makeup and hairstyles, choose energy and love the person staring back at you in the mirror. Use this information throughout the chapters as you enjoy the process of discovering your personality style your way!

KIM MITTELSTADT
KM Impressions, LLC

(210) 655-image
kim@kmimpressions.com
www.kmimpressions.com

Internationally-certified image coach, personal color analyst and CORE personality profile facilitator, Kim has brought hands-on experience to the needs of her clients since 1985. As owner and director of KM Impressions Image and Makeup Studio, and a member of the Association of Image Consultants International, she provides personal instruction in all aspects of makeup application and image development for teens and adults. She awakens your potential and helps you achieve self-confidence and faith in your own abilities, virtually ensuring your success. Her holistic approach to image development takes into consideration the whole person, creating head-to-soul beauty. Her Life Success Program for teens and adults is guaranteed to change lives.

Kim is a specialist in media, fashion and airbrush makeup application. As a licensed cosmetologist, her work has been showcased in magazines and print and on television, as well as on the covers of music CDs, on fashion runways, in pageants and more. She has organized numerous fashion shows, has trained hundreds of makeup artists in the art of airbrushing, traditional and custom-blending makeup techniques, and she assists others in starting up their own mineral cosmetic businesses.

Enhance Your Image with Color

Your Secret to Wardrobe and Makeup Harmony

By Dawn Stebbing

When you walk into a room, what do people see first? If you said your face, you are correct. Your face is what people look at first and will remember most. First impressions are very important and you only get seconds to make one. Choosing colors to enhance your image will help with that first impression.

Why is color so important? Color is an element of art and we see color first!

When you walk into a store, you see the mannequins dressed up with their outfits on and accessorized from head to toe and you say, "WOW, I want that outfit!" You often don't think about the color of the outfit and whether it would look good on you. You are just so intrigued by the work of art and how it all works together that you don't consider how it would look on your body. When this happens, ask yourself:

1. Is that a color that will bring out my best features—my eyes, hair and skin tone?

2. Is the color too bold for my body type?

3. Would people see my face first or my clothes first?

When you get dressed in the morning, you are a walking billboard of your own art. Sometimes you do a great job and sometimes not so great. How would you like to always look great? How would you like to go to your closet every day and not have to worry about what you are going to wear today? Having a color analysis done by a professional image consultant could save you a lot of time and money and take a lot of the guesswork out of getting dressed in the morning.

Some of you may remember back in the '80s, there were consultants everywhere doing color analysis by season—Spring, Summer, Fall and Winter. You would invite your friends to come to your home and the consultant would do everyone's colors. Each person would receive a pre-made set of colors. Some consultants today still use that method and that is okay. However, with those generic packets, I believe some people can get stuck in a rut, thinking they can only wear certain colors, and in some seasons, they may not find their colors at all.

With my clients, I use a different method that uses many colors to create a color fan. This fan is made up of "paddles" of color swatches individually chosen for them.

In my color training, I was taught that we are all unique in our own way. We all have different hair colors, different eye colors and different skin colors, and that is what makes us unique.

Thus, when I do a client's color analysis, I use many different color swatches. We start off with your eye color; you will end up with a paddle with just your unique eye color on it. Then we will analyze your hair color. This one can be a bit challenging, because many of us have our hair colored. When analyzing your hair, I will look at your natural underlying color and take into consideration your highlights and any other colors you may have.

Next we will look at your skin tone. This is best done without any makeup, as it will distract from your natural coloring. Once we have decided on your melanin—or beige—skin tone, we will determine your hemoglobin tone (that is the redness of your skin). You have natural red tones to your skin that determine which shades of red will be good on you. This will help you select your blush and lipstick colors. Now you have four paddles with your eye color, hair color, skin color and red tones.

With these colors as a base, we complete the rest of your fan by selecting colors that work best with your overall body colors. When we have finished, you will have a fan with 16 to 18 paddles of your personalized colors.

Black May Not Be Your Best Neutral

Most of us have black in our closets, whether it is our best neutral color or not. What do I mean by that? When you get your color fan done, look to see if you have any black in your fan. If not, it may not be one of your best colors. For example, if you have blonde hair and blue eyes, your best neutral would likely be khaki, tan or beige. If you have red hair and brown eyes, your best neutral would be brown or khaki.

Although black is not for everyone, I find that most of us have black in our closet or can't image ourselves without several wardrobe staples in black. I get it—I live in Minnesota and it can be dirty, wet, cold and sloppy six months out of the year here. In this type of climate, most people gravitate toward black. This is understandable because:

1. It hides a lot of dirt and you can get a lot of wear out of it.
2. It is easy to grab when you are in a hurry.
3. Mixing and matching is easy to do when you are in a jam.
4. It doesn't take much thought.
5. Nearly everyone has black and white in their wardrobe.

If black is not in your color fan and you just have to wear it, then wear it on the bottom and not next to your face, where it can make you look pale or washed-out. The good news is, black is classic and works well in a little black dress for a special occasion. You can pair it with a scarf or shawl in your eye color or your best metallic purse or shoes to make it work for you.

Tip: Avoid wearing black next to your face unless you have the strength of natural coloring to handle it.

White

White is another color I am asked about a lot.

White is the brightest color that attracts light and thus is very attention-getting. While not everyone can wear bright white, everybody will have some version of white in their color fan. White can be soft and elegant.

A rule of thumb is that your whites shouldn't be whiter than your teeth. I recently saw a commercial about teeth whitening featuring a bride in a white dress. Her teeth were yellowed and all you could see was her yellow teeth when she smiled. That will show up in pictures, so be aware of this when buying white blouses, shirts or any white you wear next to your face. After all, we can't all have perfectly white teeth.

Tip: Avoid wearing white as a complete outfit in the evening, unless you are next to the Equator and want to look and feel cool.

Reds

While red can be a challenging color, when you are working with your color fan, you will have lots of reds from which to choose. Most reds we see are Christmas red, blood red or orange-reds, which are great on some people, but are not what most people look good in every day. That is why I like working with a color analysis system. Instead of looking at a few common shades of red, we are looking at many shades from light, warm pinks to dark, cool reds. There are so many variations of red that there are bound to be a few in which we do look great.

Let us take red hair, for example. There are so many different shades of red hair and each one of them can go with different colored eyes. What is unique about redheads is that they can be a warm red with lots of yellow undertones to their skin or a cool red with pink undertones to their skin. Most redheads find shopping to be a challenge because they can be limited to a narrow range of colors. That is okay, because you will always look your best with the colors that look the best on you—making limited color choice a small price to pay. Redheads are beautiful when they are wearing colors that best suit them.

The reds in your color fan will be customized to enhance your hair color, skin tone and eye coloring. You will have two or three paddles of reds from which to choose, which will make your shopping experience more enjoyable—and it will save you time and money in the long run.

Tip: Avoid wearing red when meeting your future in-laws—you will scare them.

The Psychology of Colors

I have found that color has a lot of emotional and physical impact drawn to it. Colors in general change how we feel on any given day. Color can also indicate positive attributes and negative attributes. I prefer the positive connections with them.

When we are happy, we tend to dress in brighter colors and clothes that make us feel great. These colors tend to be white, yellow, orange, blue and pink. When it is gloomy outside and we are not feeling quite ourselves, we tend to wear darker clothing in black, grey and brown.

You will find that colors have a psychology around them that can be either positive or negative.

Let's take a look at some of the positives:

White. Pure, clean, fresh. White is great when worn against dark shades, such as navy, charcoal or black. The high contrast projects authority.

Black. Formal, sophisticated, mysterious, strong. Wearing black can be a sign of respect.

Red. Upbeat, confident, assertive, exciting. Choose red for occasions when you want to be recognized or to catch someone's eye.

Yellow. Cheerful, hopeful, active, uninhibited. Yellow is good to wear when you want to cheer yourself up, particularly on a dreary day.

Avoid wearing yellow to a business meeting unless you want to stand out.

Orange. Vitality, fun, enthusiasm, sociability. Orange is good if your skin, hair and eye coloring can support it.

Avoid wearing orange in any business situation; orange is the least professional color.

Pink. Feminine, gentle, accessible, non-threatening. Pink is great to complement a business suit when worn in a blouse or scarf.

Avoid wearing pink if you plan to discuss a promotion with your boss.

Blue. Peaceful, trustworthy, constant, orderly. The deepest blues project more authority.

Avoid wearing blue when making a creative pitch in PR, advertising, design or marketing. Blue and creativity are not generally felt to be synonymous.

Green. Self-reliant, tenacious, nurturing, dependable. When you are feeling overstressed and overtired, green can make you feel better.

Avoid wearing green when you are fundraising.

Brown. Earthy, homey, gregarious. This is the least threatening color to others.

Avoid wearing brown when meeting with friends who have "personal problems," as they will pour their hearts out to you.

Grey. Respectable, neutral, balanced. In business, grey is the safest option for a suit and also for a job interview.

Avoid wearing grey when you want to make things happen. Grey will hold you back from being a catalyst.

How Aging Affects Our Coloring

As we age, our skin tone, hair and eye colors soften and lose intensity. Our society seems to dictate that when men go grey, they look distinguished, while women with grey hair are considered old-looking. Women have to work harder on their looks to keep a youthful appearance.

I have a friend who often asked me my opinion of her hair, whether she should continue coloring it or let it go grey. At the time, she was over 50 percent grey underneath the colored hair. I took into consideration what she does for a living and who her clientele would be. She has her own business and her clientele would be mostly men and some women. I suggested she continue to color her hair and she asked why. Here's my response:

1. You will look more professional.

2. You will seem more polished.

3. You will command more respect.

4. You will feel much better about getting dressed in the morning.

5. You will attract more clients.

If you are wondering why this is—again, society dictates how we should look in the business world. I am not saying that grey hair is unprofessional. It all depends on the color of grey, how well it looks on you and how you will be perceived in the work world.

Makeup

I can't stress enough what a huge role makeup plays in your appearance. Are you someone who can't stand to wear makeup? In my years of working with women who dislike makeup, I have found that most of them hate the feel of it. Also, they do not know what colors look good on them, they do not want to take the time to put it on or they feel like a clown when they are made up.

Did you know when an artist paints a picture, she always starts with a fresh canvas? Your face is like the artist's canvas. Your best makeup results are achieved when you prepare your skin first with quality skin care products, including a moisturizer that absorbs into your skin and does not give you a greasy appearance. This will help your makeup go on much more easily and cleanly.

In selecting makeup colors, a good makeup artist will look at the canvas she has prepared and take into consideration the highlights of your hair color, your unique eye color, the pigment of your lips and the natural glow of your cheeks. She starts working with your best features by mixing colors to enhance your beauty, not cover it up. Having your color fan with you will help her select the makeup colors that best work for you.

Once you have achieved the look you have always wanted, it is time to put it into action. Practice makes perfect. Although I have been putting makeup on for years, I still find I am continually trying new techniques and colors. Do not be afraid of color. If you are uncertain about a color, always ask a professional for an opinion; he or she will help you, not criticize you. When you achieve the look you desire, your makeup and wardrobe will be in harmony. Work with a professional makeup artist or color consultant. This professional will guide you in looking your best for years to come. For more about makeup techniques, see Brenda Azevedo's chapter, *Wake Up Your Makeup,* on page 121.

Color is so important in our everyday lives. Once you have worked with your image consultant and received your fan, you can start shopping for clothes in colors that harmonize with you. Eventually, you will have many wonderful options in your wardrobe from which to choose. It could take up to two years for your closet to look like your color fan and that is okay. In the meantime, your image consultant can show you ways to adapt your existing wardrobe with scarves, jewelry and other techniques. As your closet begins to look more and more like your color fan, it will be easy to mix and match colors you would have never put together before. Why does it work that way? Because it is personalized for you. No one else will have the same colors in her color fan as you do. You are unique—remember that.

Now how do you feel walking into a room? By enhancing your image with color, you will look good and feel good. When we feel good, we perform better. When we perform better, bigger and better things come our way. So call your professional image consultant and work with her to customize your personal color fan. You can start saving time, saving money and looking your best today and every day you walk out your door.

DAWN STEBBING
Image Evolution

Authentic and lasting beauty:
the kind that can't be bought off the rack

(651) 307-0342
dawn@imageevolutionmn.com
www.imageevolutionmn.com

Dawn lives in Vadnais Heights, Minnesota. As a professional in the beauty industry since 1987, she continues to deliver outer beauty to countless women and understands that refreshing their public image can lift their inner spirits.

Through Dawn's own personal journey and search for inspiration, she learned that personal style is only part of the beauty equation. By uncovering her own buried passions, dreams, talents and powers, Dawn discovered her authentic self and realized that true beauty is holistic—a combination of inner passion and outer styling to match. Through Image Evolution, Dawn helps clients discover their own inner power and personal styles so they can harness and cultivate their authentic beauty.

Dawn has drive and enthusiasm when working with individuals and groups, as she shares her skills in color analysis, style and fit analysis, wardrobe audits and coaching with the Core Passion™ assessment. Dawn believes in giving her clients a "complete package" from the inside out and the outside in.

Be True to Your Shape
A Guide to Dressing for Your Body Type

By Johonna Duckworth

The first two years of my fashion career were spent working in retail. Of the women I assisted in the designer apparel department, many of them—whether they were petite, missy or plus-size—had one thing in common: they did not know how to dress for their body type. Their lack of knowledge was often displayed in their purchasing decisions that resulted in clothing being returned because of a poor fit. I quickly learned that a woman's size does not necessarily coincide with her actual body type. From that point on, I made it my mission to learn the different body types so I could provide better service to those who need guidance.

> *"The dress must follow the body of a woman,*
> *not the body following the shape of the dress."*
> —Hubert de Givenchy, French fashion designer

The key to achieving impeccable style is first to discover your body's shape. From plus-size to petite, every woman has a particular body type. Because no two women are shaped exactly the same, use the following illustrations as a general guide to determine the basis of your body type.

TRIANGLE. A woman with a Triangle body shape typically has narrow shoulders, a defined waistline and wider hips.

Your style challenge: Because your lower body is heavier than your upper body, you want to draw attention away from your thighs and bottom.

Reveal: Neckline and small waistline
Conceal: Large bottom and wide hips

Must-haves

- **Pants.** Dark-colored, straight- or wide-legged pants are best. Boot-cut jeans will balance the hips.

- **Jackets.** Select structured fabrics with strong shoulder lines. Puffy sleeves will help balance the shoulders with the hips.

- **Tops.** Collared shirts with structure. Square-neck shirts will balance the hips.

- **Skirts.** Wear solid-color or small-patterned A-line skirts. Skirts hemmed at the knee and draped easily over the hips will look best.

- **Shapewear.** Triangle body shapes need control in the bottom, hips and thighs. Select shapewear that has control from the waist to the mid-thigh or to just below the knee. A push-up bra will add balance to a smaller bustline.

Style Tips

- Petites with Triangle body types are advised to avoid wearing floor-length dresses and skirts. These hide your legs and make you look shorter.

- Plus-size Triangles can opt for tonal or monochromatic dressing, which gives the illusion of elongation. Use colors and textures to reveal the best parts of your figure, and avoid clothing that is baggy or too tight.

Fashion Fact

According to a May 7, 2006, CBS News story, the skirt is the second oldest women's garment in history. Only loin cloths pre-date it.

INVERTED TRIANGLE. A woman with an Inverted Triangle shape typically has broad shoulders, narrow hips and an undefined waist.

Your style challenge: Make the width of your broad shoulders balance with your small waist and hips.

Reveal: Small hips and narrow thighs
Conceal: Areas above the waist to prevent looking top-heavy

Must-haves

- **Pants.** Fitted pants with straight legs and diagonal side pockets look great on an inverted triangle. Pants with pocket flaps on the back will make the bottom look fuller.

- **Jackets.** Shorter jackets with princess seams and jackets that flare out slightly at the hips are best. Belted V-neck cardigans, as well as jackets and tops, will vertically slim top-heaviness.

- **Skirts.** Wear skirts that add volume to the hips. Pleated and tulip skirts will add width to the hips. Knee-length skirts with contoured waistbands and side pockets are also good.

- **Dresses.** Corset-style dresses will give great definition to the waist. Shift dresses, bias cut and tunic dresses will help to balance broad shoulders with narrow hips.
- **Shapewear.** Inverted Triangle body shapes carry most of their weight above the waist and need control in the midriff section as well as a bra that lifts and supports fuller breasts.

Style Tips

- Inverted Triangle women are advised to avoid double-breasted tops and jackets.
- Avoid pencil skirts if you have a fuller bustline—slim skirts will over-emphasize your broad shoulders and make you look top-heavy.

Fashion Fact

Numerous studies have estimated that more than 80 percent of women are wearing the wrong bra size.

RECTANGLE. A woman with a Rectangle shape has a straight line from her shoulder to her hips. In most cases, the shoulders, bust, waist and hips are all similar in size with no real defined waist.

Your style challenge: Although Rectangles are usually easy to dress, you want to add volume to a flat bottom.

Reveal: Arms, legs and hips
Conceal: Undefined waist

Must-haves

- **Pants.** Boot-cut and straight-legged pants bring balance to thin legs.

- **Jackets.** Round-collar jackets and jackets with princess seams that skim the waist will give definition to your waist. Belted cardigans, jackets and tops will also help to define your waist.
- **Skirts.** A-line skirts will create an illusion of curvy hips. Trumpet-style skirts will also add curves to your hips.
- **Tops.** Tops with breast pockets will conceal a smaller bustline. Button-down shirts with princess seams will add definition to the waist.
- **Shapewear.** Boy shorts or panty girdles work well with Rectangle body types. A long-line bra will give definition to smaller breasts and help define the waist.

Style Tips

- Petite Rectangles will look best when wearing dark-colored, straight-legged pants with pointed-toe shoes to elongate the legs.
- Adding a wide belt to a jacket or top can help bring definition to an undefined waist.

Fashion Fact

Stores.org reports that $28 billion a year of merchandise is returned to stores because of poor fit.

HOURGLASS: A woman with an Hourglass body shape has equal measurements for hips and bust with a smaller waistline.

Your style challenge: Conceal wide hips and full thighs.

Reveal: Small waistline, bustline and shapely calves.
Conceal: Large hips and full thighs

Must-haves

- **Pants.** Choose a flat-front, solid-color pant with flared legs. Boot-cut and wide-legged trouser jeans with a little stretch will conceal large hips and fuller thighs—and they feel great!

- **Jackets.** Wearing fitted jackets that stop just above the hipline will emphasize a small waistline. Adding a small to medium belt to a jacket or lightweight knit cardigan also draws the eye to the small waist.

- **Skirts.** A-line skirts will conceal a round bottom and large hips.

- **Dresses.** Fitted sheath dresses will flatter your curves. A wrap dress will reveal your smaller waistline and equalize shoulder and hip measurements.

- **Shapewear.** Hourglass body types need control and support in the bottom, hips and thighs in addition to a well-fitted bra to avoid sagging breasts.

Style Tips

- Plus-size Hourglass body types look best when wearing wrap-style dresses and tops that show off the bustline and hug the waist.

- Be careful to avoid pants and shirts that are too tight. Choose soft fabrics that skim over your curves.

Fashion Fact

A 2005 study of over 6,000 women carried out by researchers at North Carolina State University found that 46 percent were "bananas" (Rectangles), just over 20 percent were "pears" (Triangles), just under 14 percent were "apples" (Ovals), and 8 percent were Hourglass-shaped.

OVAL. A woman with an Oval body type is considered to be round in general and has an undefined waistline. Ovals tend to have stomachs that are positioned low.

Your style challenge: Conceal sloping shoulders and bring definition to a large abdomen.

Reveal: Thin hips
Conceal: Lower large, round abdomen and sloping shoulders

Must-haves

- **Pants.** Choose a flat-front, solid-color pant with flared legs. Boot-cut and wide-legged trouser jeans with a little stretch will conceal large hips and fuller thighs—and they feel great!

- **Jackets.** Wearing fitted jackets that stop just above the hipline will emphasize a small waistline. Adding a small to medium belt to a jacket or lightweight knit cardigan also draws the eye to the small waist.

- **Skirts.** A-line skirts will conceal a round bottom and large hips.

- **Dresses.** Fitted sheath dresses will flatter your curves. A wrap dress will reveal your smaller waistline and equalize shoulder and hip measurements.

- **Shapewear.** Hourglass body types need control and support in the bottom, hips and thighs in addition to a well-fitted bra to avoid sagging breasts.

Style Tip

- Oval shapes will want to avoid tucked-in tops, which bring unwanted attention to the midriff.

Fashion Fact

Women under five feet, four inches tall are considered petite by the fashion industry, whether they are size 0 or 24.

DIAMOND. A woman with a Diamond body shape normally has narrow shoulders and hips with a wide, undefined waist. A Diamond's stomach tends to be positioned high.

Your style challenge: Define your high waist and conceal fuller thighs.

Reveal: Neckline; emphasize shoulders
Conceal: Waistline and full upper thighs

Must-haves

- **Pants.** Wearing straight-legged pants and pants with flared legs and higher pockets will elongate your legs and balance narrow hips. Boot-cut jeans with side pockets and a little spandex will look good and feel great.

- **Jackets.** Choose single-button jackets with shoulder pads and a boxy style. This will conceal your waist and balance your shoulders.

- **Dresses.** Two-piece, loosely flowing dresses will conceal a high-positioned stomach. Adding a jacket or sweater will help define your narrow shoulders.

- **Skirts.** A-line, knee-length skirts will de-emphasize your waist and narrow hips.

- **Shapewear.** Diamond body shapes need control in the midriff area. A high-waisted girdle will provide the needed support in the midriff.

Style Tips

• Diamond shapes will want to avoid wearing double-breasted jackets and belted shirts, which draw the eye to the waist.

• Dressing in monochromatic tones will give an elongated look and help minimize the appearance of a large waistline.

Fashion Fact

According to the 2003 Size USA survey, the average American woman is 5 feet, 4 inches tall and wears a size 14.

For the Men in Your Life

Although this book is for women, you may have a man in your life who could use some image advice. When it comes to everyday style, most fashion self-help guides neglect men. It is just as important for a man to know his body type as it is for a woman to know hers. A well-dressed man is fully aware of the shape of his body and knows his style limitations.

As an image consultant who consults with men and as the wife of a former college athlete, I know that men, like women, also come in all shapes and sizes and often have similar shopping challenges. The way a man's body is shaped does not have to detract from his sense of style. For every man, there is a style that complements his body type. The following information is designed to help you guide your man to great fit and style.

INVERTED TRIANGLE. This man typically has broad shoulders with a narrow waist, typical of men with athletic builds.

His style challenge: to make the width of his broad shoulders balance with his small waist.

Style Tips

Suggest he wear:

- Jackets with shoulders that are light or unpadded.
- Suits that are cut for athletic bodies.
- Suiting separates and sports coats with trousers.
- Pants at his natural waist to elongate his legs.
- Pants with pleats. They will camouflage the bulk.
- Boot-cut jeans. They balance out his wide shoulders.

Suggest he avoid wearing:

- Double-breasted suits, because they add to the bulky muscle-man look that is common with men who lift weights.
- Skinny jeans. They do not balance his narrow waist and his wide shoulders.
- Tight spandex shirts. These shirts might show off his athletic upper body, but they won't balance out his narrow waist with his wide shoulders.

TRIANGLE. This man normally has narrow shoulders, a wider waist and a heavier lower body.

His style challenge: to draw attention away from his waist, thighs and bottom.

Style Tips

Suggest he wear:

- Jackets with shoulder pads to balance his shoulders and hip area.
- Double-breasted jackets to balance his narrow shoulders.

- Flat-front pants or straight-legged jeans to camouflage a larger lower body.

Suggest he avoid wearing:

- Shirts with seams wider than his shoulders
- Belted trench coats. They will make his waist look wider.
- Boot-cut or low-rise jeans with pocket details. They draw attention to his wider hips and waist.

RECTANGLE. This man has equal shoulder and waist measurements. In general, a Rectangle-shaped man is easy to dress. He can wear most clothing off the rack with little or no altering.

His style challenge: to add volume to a flat bottom.

Style Tips

Suggest he wear:

- Jackets with shoulder pads to strengthen the look of his shoulders.
- V-neck and button-down shirts to balance a boxy frame.
- Boot–cut, low-rise jeans with pocket details, which will elongate his legs and give definition to a flat bottom.

Suggest he avoid wearing:

- Skinny jeans because they just don't look good on Rectangle men!

ROUND. This man usually has sloping shoulders and a high, round stomach. Some men with a Round body shape have developed some additional breast tissue.

His style challenge is to draw attention away from his waist or his chest.

Style Tips

Suggest he wear:

- Pants with wider legs to balance his wider torso.

- A single-breasted jacket with two to four buttons. Jackets with belts overemphasize a round waist.

- Belts with his pants.

- Loose-fitting cardigan sweaters and button-down vests that fall below the stomach to conceal a wider waist.

- Shirts outside his pants when wearing casual attire.

Suggest he avoid wearing:

- Double-breasted jackets. They draw attention to a round stomach.

- Horizontal stripes or busy patterns. They make him look wider than he is.

- Skinny/slim pants. Just because "skinny" is in the title doesn't mean they will make him look that way!

- Shirts tucked in; it draws the eye to a wider waist. Fitted shirts and sweaters also draw the eye to the waist.

Whether you are a woman who is on an effective weight loss plan, or you are with a man who gained 20 pounds two years ago, it is important for both of you to dress for your current size and shape. Wearing clothing that is too big or too tight is not flattering to any body type. Buying a few staple items in your actual size will encourage you to continue on any weight loss program. Adding clothes to his wardrobe that fit his increased size will help him look and feel better.

Now that you know your body shape, invest in items of higher quality, especially when concealing problem areas. Shopping for clothing that fits your body shape does not have to break the bank. Avoid over-spending on trendy items that will go out of style soon. Investing in the highest quality clothing your budget can afford will keep you from having to replace staple items often. Remember, impeccable style has nothing to do with your body size and everything to do with the perfect fit! Be true to your shape.

JOHONNA DUCKWORTH
Creative Images

*Creating positive first impressions
that last beyond introductions*

(414) 687-5999
johonna@yourcre8tiveimage.com
www.yourcre8tiveimage.com

While building her career as a technology connoisseur, Johonna witnessed first-hand the impact that a professional image has on upward mobility. Cultivating her personal shopping skills at the exclusive chain of Marshall Field & Company stores, a former subsidiary of The May Department Stores Company, Johonna officially launched Creative Images LLC, a full-service impression management consulting company, in 2006.

With more than 10 years of experience in providing wardrobe solutions and life skills coaching, Johonna has selflessly offered her experience, personality and style as a consultant and mentor to men and women both young and old. Through her informative workshops and makeovers, she uses the outward expression of "image" only as a topical solution in helping clients improve their overall self-concept and quality of life.

Johonna holds a bachelor's degree in computer information systems from Grambling State University and double associate degrees in fashion marketing and retail management from Milwaukee Area Technical College. Johonna is also a certified Life Skills Coach and serves on the Board of Directors for The Milwaukee Outreach Center, where she teaches communication and job readiness skills.

Posture Is Paramount!

By Cindy Ann Peterson, AICI FLC

No amount of high fashion can make up for a lifetime of poor posture.

I never thought that while my friends were being fitted for bras, I would be getting fitted for a back brace. As a young girl, I always had great posture—my shoulders were straight and in line with my hips. Then I was diagnosed with scoliosis, a type of curvature of the spine. This meant I had to wear a Milwaukee brace that went from my hips to my chin to keep the curve from progressing. I wore the brace for seven years, twenty-three hours a day.

It was in fifth grade that I started to learn about the spine and how posture can affect a person. While I could not control my spinal curve through exercise, practicing good posture has been a lifelong lesson for me. That is why I am passionate about good posture and why I want to help you. Good posture is important for health reasons, as well as for your appearance, because it reflects your personal attitude. More than attitude, posture has also been used throughout history to communicate one's status in society.

Posture and Social Status

During the 18th century in European and American society, aspects including station in life, status and dress could easily identify those of financial means. In fact, the garments of this era would hold the wearer in a position that would support and require proper posture. Women, and sometimes men, wore stays in order to shape the torso. Among the more privileged, even children wore stays since people believed these improved their posture and enhanced straight spinal growth. Certain movements were constrained by the cut and design of many garments, including details of the sleeve and back that would hold the person in proper posture.

Lord Chesterfield, an author of instructional books of the time, wrote, "If a man walks well, presents himself well in company, wears his hat well, moves his head properly and his arms gracefully, it is almost all that is necessary." It is still relevant today to project a confident image through good body posture.

Posture Reflects Your Attitude

How you carry yourself speaks volumes about how you feel about yourself. Our nonverbal behavior (including posture) gives away our inner personality and reflects our inner attitude. Your posture can have a great deal of influence on your personal presentation and image, revealing your attitude toward yourself and others.

> *"A good stance and posture reflect a proper state of mind."*
> —Morihei Ueshiba,
> Japanese founder of Aikido and martial arts master

What do others think of you the first time they meet you? Did you know it takes only a few seconds to make a first impression on someone? Have you ever stopped to consider how many first impressions you get to make on each person you meet? Yes, just one. Why not make it the best presentation possible?

People with good posture are seen as:	People with poor posture are seen as:
Confident	Messy/Disheveled
Reliable	Unorganized
Organized	Unprofessional
Businesslike	Disengaged
Poised	Uninterested
Punctual	Lackadaisical

Confident posture gets you noticed for all the right reasons. Great style and great posture go hand in hand. Proper posture sends a positive image message since 90 percent of all communication occurs through body language and how you carry yourself. Executive etiquette and civility expert Deborah King, AICI CIP, believes, "Correct posture is not rigid, but upright, and supports the body as it moves. The overall effect is one of effortless grace and confident movement."

Why Good Posture?

Think of good posture as your body's projection of a positive message to those you meet. Good posture is the correct alignment of body parts supported by the right amount of muscle tension. It does not take the striking pose of a high-fashion model or the strict stance of someone in uniform to earn respect and admiration.

There are many benefits to maintaining good posture. Some of these are:

- You instantly look 10 pounds lighter.
- You experience better health throughout your lifetime.
- You look more youthful.
- You have more energy.
- You stand taller.
- You exude self-confidence.
- There is an illusion of a larger chest by lifting the ribcage.
- Your clothing fits you better.
- People see you shine in a positive light.

Additionally, good posture can be beneficial to your health:

- It can prevent backaches and muscular pain.

- It promotes larger lung capacity, bringing in more oxygen to the blood and enabling improved speech and breathing.

- It may help prevent abnormal wearing of joints.

- You elongate and open up the spaces between the vertebrae, allowing more oxygen to get into the discs and increasing your range of motion.

What May Cause Poor Posture?

In addition to medical problems, other things can contribute to poor posture. If you have been injured, you may hold your body in a particular way to compensate for the injury, or to avoid pain when walking. After the injury heals, the compensating posture may continue. Stress can also lead to poor posture because it causes you to breathe more shallowly, which leads to slumping. Working conditions at the computer and long seated sessions can lead to weakness and pronounced posture problems.

Adolescents experiencing a growth spurt can develop posture problems, although this is usually more of a problem for girls than for boys. Because of young girls' early growth spurt, their skeletons are not maturing as quickly as they are gaining muscle mass. Everything grows so fast and their center of gravity keeps changing.

As young women develop breasts, some, because of embarrassment, slouch and hunch their shoulders. Others want to make a strong impression with their "newly developed friends" and will flaunt them, causing a swayback from pushing out their chests. Both can cause a problem going into adulthood.

Your Personal Center of Gravity

Healthy posture is based on natural positions that balance and support your skeletal system's curves and weight-bearing abilities against the force of gravity. To help you think about your center of gravity, try this visualization exercise. Imagine a wire at the top of your head, running down through the center of the neck, down the center of your torso and down each leg. Imagine, further, that this wire is pulling you up from the top of your head, like a puppet. When the wire is loose or lax, you fall into misalignment. When the wire is pulled taut, your head is held high and straight and your body is aligned—from your head down through your back and legs to your toes.

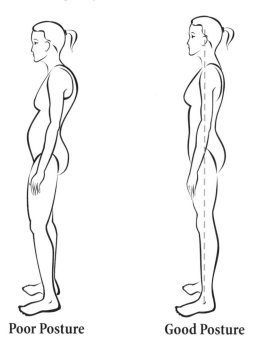

Poor Posture   **Good Posture**

The American Physical Therapy Association's publication, *The Secret of Good Posture: A Physical Therapist's Perspective,* published in 1998, notes that good posture, as seen from the side in the diagram above, shows your ear, shoulder, hip and ankle to be in line with one other. Poor posture, in the same view, shows the head to be in front of or behind this center of gravity, causing the upper back to hunch or the lower back to arch too much.

How is your posture? You can use a video camera to find out. Use the camera's viewpoint and observe what others are really seeing.

- Set up a video camera and tape yourself walking, sitting and standing.
- Check to see if you are keeping your center of gravity in line.
- Have a lined paper on the wall so you can evaluate if you are standing, walking and sitting straight. Do this from front, side and back views.

Chris Fulkerson, a co-author of *Inspired Style,* published by PowerDynamics Publishing in 2010, says, "Old habits are hard to break. You need to establish a cue or trigger to jog your memory to check your posture periodically. The telephone and the mirror are good triggers. Each time the phone rings, check your posture, or each time you pass a mirror, check your posture."

Walking Tall

What does your walk say about you? Are you polished, poised and professional? Here are some tips to help you walk with perfect posture. Prepare to walk with style and finesse!

- **Head.** Hold it high. Remember the wire pulling from the top of your head? Keep your head relatively still, not looking from side to side.
- **Chin.** Keep it parallel to the floor. If you drop your head to look down, the wire will break. Think elegant and graceful!
- **Shoulders.** Relax them, allowing them to go down and back.

- **Arms.** Relax and allow them to move comfortably at your side, moving mainly from the shoulder, not the elbow. Your thumbs should be leading your arm, not your knuckles.

- **Hands.** Gently touch your fingertips to your thighs, then release. Keep your hands in a soft, natural position.

- **Chest.** Posture is kept up and open. Keeping your shoulders back will help with the chest posture.

  Stretch the chest and relax the upper back by standing in a door way, placing a hand on either side of the door frame and leaning with your upper body for at least 20 seconds. Repeat this a few times a day.

- **Abdominal muscles.** Stomach is pulled in, firm and controlled. If you need help, wear some kind of waist support. Strong stomach muscles not only look great, they also promote a strong lower back.

- **Hips.** Allow them to rotate naturally. Do not throw them, and do let them move—as women, we have that privilege. Work that skirt!

  Seat is slightly tucked beneath your hips for better control. Squeeze your bun muscles to keep your legs engaged.

- **Legs.** Adopt a gentle step. Your knees will almost fully extend as you plant each foot onto the floor. Do not lock your knees.

- **Feet.** Think like a dancer, heel to toe is the way to go. Using your back leg, push yourself forward.

Remember it takes 21 days to change a behavioral pattern—so start practicing your posture while walking today.

Posture Power

If you are interviewing for a job and you say you are very interested in the position, but your posture suggests an uncaring attitude, the interviewers will probably doubt you. Catherine Graham Bell, AICI

CIP, reflects in *Managing Your Image Potential: Creating Good Impressions in Business,* published in 2001 by Prime Impressions, that "Your visual image speaks volumes . . . when your body language contradicts your words, your credibility will be questioned." Poor posture shows uncertainty and a lack of confidence and ability. Good posture conveys confidence and an air of capability.

A great attitude toward your approach to an interview—demonstrated by your good posture—is everything.

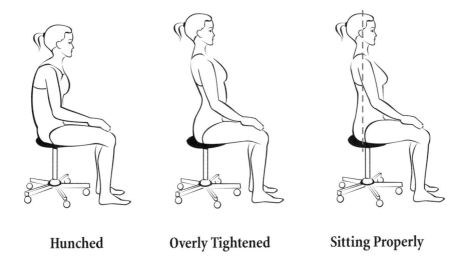

| Hunched | Overly Tightened | Sitting Properly |

Sit Up Straight!

It is important that you keep your good posture while sitting—just like your mom always told you. Approach the chair from the side and let your legs touch the back of the chair so you won't have to turn and look for the chair. Lower yourself to the edge of the chair using your thigh muscles. Now slide back into the chair. You may sit with both feet flat on the floor or you can cross your feet at the ankles, keeping your feet behind your knees. If you cross your legs, cross them in the direction you are sitting. The legs should be nearly parallel and next to each other, without swinging. If in doubt, then just do not cross them. Sit tall, without slouching. Rest your hands in your lap or on the armrests.

To rise from a seated position, uncross your legs or ankles, placing both feet flat on the floor. Using your arms, push yourself forward and upward, and then use your thigh muscles to push yourself up as you maintain perfect posture.

Help Is Available

In all areas of your life, striving for proper posture can enhance your career, style and health. If you have some posture challenges, you can dress in a way that will camouflage them. A resource I use is *The Triumph of Individual Style* by Carla Mathis and Helen Connor, published in 2002 by Fairchild Publications. Known as the "bible" of the image industry, this book provides a "body particulars overview," including an enlightened approach to understanding body types, color and personal style, and addresses clothing for people with posture variations.

> *"Unless some misfortune has made it impossible,*
> *everyone can have good posture."*
> —Loretta Young, American movie and television actress

For medical reasons, some teens and adults may need to wear a brace or have a surgical correction. Life is full of challenges, seen and unseen, so to look and feel great, you must hold your head up each day and project your inner confidence .

Habitually poor posture contributes to back pain and may indicate a bone deformity or other underlying medical condition. I am lucky to have benefitted from medical intervention by the leaders in a major study of the adolescent spine, Dr. Robert B. Winter and Dr. John H. Moe. If you have back pain or a problem with your posture, be sure to have it checked by your doctor.

If your posture issue does not warrant medical attention, there are many types of undergarments and supports to help you achieve better posture. In addition to corset-style garments for daytime wear, there are upper or lower back supports that may be worn to bed to allow the back to rest in proper alignment. Sleeping with a pillow between the knees will help to keep the hips aligned and keep the spine in relaxed balance. A small rolled towel or roll pillow placed at the waist will keep the lower back in line.

To develop your own posture support, explore using some type of core strengthening training, like Pilates or yoga. Find a program that works for your needs and allows you to create the body you deserve.

When you fine-tune your core body strength, you learn to maintain great posture for life. It is important to keep your shoulders straight and in line with your hips—and every time the phone rings, do a posture check!

By taking good care of your posture now, you will enjoy and savor lifelong health benefits and beauty.

"I want to get old gracefully. I want to have good posture,
I want to be healthy and be an example to my children."
—Gordon Sumner, aka Sting,
English singer-songwriter, actor and philanthropist

Posture Really Is Paramount

A strong, confident person can rule the room with knowledge, personal style, attitude and great posture. Your posture is the key to your personal and professional foundation.

You can spend a great deal of time, money and energy acquiring an incredible wardrobe. However, without good posture, the effect or image you are trying to achieve will be lost. Use proper posture to realize your professional image potential because . . .

Great posture never goes out of style!

CINDY ANN PETERSON, AICI FLC
Couture Design and
Professional Image Management

*Great posture is the foundation
that always fits.*

(703) 593-5827
cap@cindyannpeterson.com
www.cindyannpeterson.com

Cindy Ann Peterson is an independent fashion and design consultant specializing in couture. Her interest and passion is the creation of a complete client package by dovetailing her couture skills with image consulting, creating a unique synthesis of fashion and image transformation.

Cindy Ann is a designer, author, speaker and radio and television spokesperson on sewing and style. Her works have been published in nationally recognized magazines. She has also been recognized for her creations in national-level competition skating events, as well as clothing for the disabled. In 1994, she was tailor-on-call to President Clinton at the Asian Pacific Economic Conference.

Cindy Ann received her BS degree from the University of Wisconsin-Stout in apparel, textiles and design, and is currently studying with the Fashion Institute of Technology in New York City. Peterson is Universal Style-certified by Alyce Parsons.

Her unique expertise has created a broad client base in the greater Washington, D.C. area, with executive-level customers from corporations and academia to U.S. Government agencies and departments. Professional memberships include: Association of Image Consultants International and The American Sewing Guild. Cindy Ann received AICI's 2010 Civility Star Award for her work on the Civility Counts Project.

Building a Personalized Capsule Wardrobe

Realize Your Dream Wardrobe Using Ready-to-Wear, Do-It-Yourself and Custom Garments

By Jana Rezucha, AICI FLC

"True elegance consists not in having a closet bursting with clothes, but rather in having a few well-chosen numbers in which one feels totally at ease."
—Coco Chanel, French fashion designer and style icon

Do you imagine a wardrobe made up of exactly the outfits that are prancing down the runway in your head? If you are like most women, you've been trying to build your dream wardrobe since before you hit your teens and have had varying degrees of success—pink and purple princess dresses aside. You just can't always find what you're looking for, or if you do find it, it rarely fits right. Yet you continue to dream of a wardrobe that is exactly what you want: Garments that you love and that fit well, are easy to mix and match and are functional for every situation in your life. Somehow your wardrobe has never seemed to work out quite right—something is always missing, and you can end up feeling frustrated, defeated and even frumpy.

There is a better way, a smarter, more affordable way to build your dream wardrobe than by just going to the mall and hoping to find the items you've imagined on your virtual runway. I've found a solution to having exactly what you want: Start thinking about building a coordinated wardrobe that includes items you buy at a store or from a catalog (ready-to-wear), as well as items that you make yourself (do-it-yourself), have altered, or enlist other people to make just for you (custom-made).

You're probably thinking "Maybe that's okay for people with plenty of disposable income, but it could never happen with my budget!" Before you dismiss the possibility, please read on and I will show you just how easy, affordable and fun it can be to make your dream wardrobe come true.

The Capsule Wardrobe Concept

Your dream wardrobe starts with the capsule concept of building a coordinated wardrobe. Building a coordinated or "capsule" wardrobe is not a new concept; in fact, designers use this principle every season to create their mix-and-match lines of clothing. The idea is that you make a mini-wardrobe out of a group of several garments that are coordinated by color and style. Typically, the mini-wardrobe will be centered around a specific function—like a work wardrobe or a casual wardrobe—though you can have a mini-wardrobe that has elements of both.

Benefits of a Capsule Wardrobe

As you build your capsule wardrobe, you will discover many benefits of constructing your wardrobe in this way. This method will:

- **Create more outfits with fewer clothes.** This is simple math—I mean really simple math. Each piece can be worn with almost every other piece, allowing you to create many new looks just by substituting a different top or pant.

- **Make wardrobe-building manageable by breaking it down into small, doable sections.** Because you are only considering a portion of your wardrobe for one primary function, the whole task feels easy to accomplish.

- **Save time when shopping.** If you've built your mini-wardrobe based on the colors brown and turquoise, you don't have to bother looking through the purples, reds, blacks and other colors on the racks. This alone will quickly eliminate about 75 percent of your choices in the store.

- **Save money.** First, you will buy fewer clothes because everything goes together and that gives you many more wearing options. Second, you will only buy what already coordinates with your other clothes. That means no more orphans that never get worn. These are often the garments hanging in your closet with the price tags still attached. Ouch!

- **Simplify your life!** Ahhhh, the Zen of having clothes that work together. You can literally reach into your closet and pick out anything because it can all be worn together. Who cares if your brown gabardine skirt is in the wash? You can still wear the shirt you picked out because you have four other choices of bottoms to wear with it. Feel the ease—it matches, it's coordinated in style, you have shoes and a belt that work with it and you love it.

Building Your Capsule Wardrobe

Now that you are convinced the capsule method is an effective and money-saving way to build a wardrobe that works, it's time for the fun part—actually building your dream wardrobe using ready-to-wear and custom garments.

Where do you start? As with most things in life, you can begin in a number of ways.

- **What you have in your closet.** This is probably the easiest way to start building your wardrobe, unless you are building a wardrobe for an entirely new function in your life. Pick an outfit, preferably a jacket or jacket-like item and a bottom piece—skirt or pant—and go from there.

- **A new outfit.** Your new outfit is a great starting point; since you just selected it, it is sure to be in the colors and style you like today.

- **A color scheme.** Another fun way to start a new wardrobe is by first choosing the color scheme for your new look. Use items from your home—like a favorite rug or vase—or pictures in magazines for inspiration.

Now that you are off to a great start, what do you do next? Plan for five or more coordinated items of clothing. Most wardrobe-building advice suggests using five to twelve pieces. One great guideline is the Perfect Wardrobe Builder™ concept as outlined in Shirley Borrelli's chapter in *Inspired Style,* published by PowerDynamics Publishing in 2010. Shirley recommends building your wardrobe based on two jackets, five bottoms and four tops.

Sample
Mini-Wardrobe

Keep the following in mind when choosing the items for your capsule. Your mini-wardrobe will function best if you:

- Choose basic pieces to start your capsule. Simple styles and shapes are the most versatile; they are easy to wear and will stay in style the longest.
- Make sure that each piece works with at least two other pieces. Ideally, every top could be worn with every bottom and every jacket could be worn with each top/bottom combination.
- Select pieces that are different from the others. How boring would it be if all of your bottoms were straight-legged pants and all your tops were cap-sleeved blouses?
- Use two main colors.
- Include an item with a print that has all the colors of your wardrobe.

Let's say you start with a brown suit from your closet; that equals one jacket and one bottom for your capsule. Now, look in your closet for garments in a coordinating color that will act as the second color in the capsule. Alternatively, if you don't see a second color in your closet, just pick a color you like that goes well with brown. Remember, we are using two main colors to build your capsule and adding coordinating colors after we've got the capsule started. As stated previously, to really get the wardrobe you've been dreaming of, use a combination of ready-to-wear and custom-sewn garments to build it. There are several things to consider when deciding which option will result in the perfect addition to your wardrobe.

Here are some sources for finding ready-to-wear or custom-made garments:

Ready-to-Wear Options

- **Department stores.** These stores carry everything from makeup to housewares, and also have a varied and wide selection of women's clothing. Because they offer so much selection, they can often be a timesaver, especially since you now know the colors and styles for which you will be shopping.

- **Boutiques or specialty stores.** The buyer for this type of smaller store is often the owner of the store; thus, the merchandise will usually reflect her taste. You can window shop at several boutiques until you find one that generally fits your style. Prices may be a little higher, and having a selection that fits your style and salespeople who know their stuff will be worth the added cost.

- **Discount stores.** From Target® to Marshall's®, these very popular stores can be a huge help for the budget-conscious. Selection changes frequently at these places, so you may have to drop in often to find something suitable. A discount store is probably a better choice for trendy items and low-cost basics than for investment pieces.

- **Catalogs or online shopping.** Anything and everything is available from a catalog or online these days. The big benefit is shopping from home 24/7; the downsides include not being able to touch and feel the merchandise or try it on for size. The item may be just as pictured and fit perfectly, or it may turn out to be a weird color and be made to fit a giant. Ordering is convenient, and returns can be a pain. Be sure to factor that in if you plan to shop using this method.

- **Resale shops.** These shops offer the ultimate in bargains, and may also be the ultimate in hit-or-miss. These consignment or thrift stores usually get one of each item, in one size only, from the person donating or consigning the piece. You may fall in love with an item only to realize that it is four sizes too small! My advice is to shop these stores when you have an open mind and no urgent clothing needs. You may go home empty-handed, and there is also the distinct possibility that you may find the best bargain ever!

Custom Options

- **Alterations specialist.** An alterations shop can change your clothes in small ways that make them perfect for you. In most cases, they will be able to shorten a hemline, take in or let out the waistband, reduce the excess fabric in a blouse and make other similar alterations. An alterations shop can also change the style of a piece somewhat—for example, change wide-legged pants to straight-legged or make an A-line skirt into a pencil style. Since each garment is unique in construction and material, be sure to discuss the possibilities with the alterations specialist before assuming what can or cannot be done—and definitely before removing the tags.

Leave the seam full at the hip.

Taper the seam to the hem.

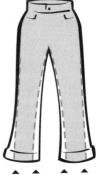

Pin at inseam and outseam to test the new width.

- **Do-it-yourself.** Making a garment yourself can be one of life's great joys. To start, find a very simple pattern and an appropriate fabric that you love. If you have never sewn a garment before, ask an experienced friend for some help. Alternatively, sewing classes are available at fabric stores, through adult education centers and even online. Or you can start even simpler. If the only thing you've ever sewn is that misshapen pillow from your junior high sewing class, here's an opportunity to sew something that will add a touch of color and variety to your capsule wardrobe: make a wardrobe-enhancing accessory like a scarf or a tote bag. Start simple and thrill yourself; your wardrobe will thank you!

- **Full-service dressmaker.** A skilled dressmaker can truly make you whatever you want or need. Have a consultation first to discuss your wishes and to see some completed projects. You may also want to ask for references. A dressmaker can cost more than buying something off the rack, but it will be worth it to get exactly what you want.

Ready-to-Wear or Custom?

When should you choose ready-to-wear or custom? In general, buy ready-to-wear when you need something in a hurry, know a brand that fits you well, and can easily get access to it. Ready-to-wear is often great for basics like T-shirts, jeans and lingerie. Consider your custom options—alterations, do-it-yourself sewing or custom dressmaking—when you have something in mind and haven't been able to find it in ready-to-wear. Let's consider some possible scenarios for each custom option:

- **You require a unique fit.** Who doesn't? Full confession: the main reason I started sewing was to get pant legs and shirt sleeves long enough for me. While fulfilling my desire to make functional tall-girl clothes, I discovered that I really loved the more creative aspects of sewing; thus my life-long addiction to sewing and all things fabric was born. Once you experience the joys of wearing clothes that really fit, you will love using the various custom options available to you.

- **Matching an old piece of clothing.** You've got a stunning mulberry tweed skirt from several years ago, but unfortunately the matching blouse has a bacon-gorgonzola burger stain front and center. The skirt is languishing in your closet. You've been looking for a replacement blouse, but that glorious mulberry color is nowhere to be found. Custom sewing to the rescue!

- **Add missing pieces.** The suit you just bought didn't have a skirt option, and you'd love to have a skirt to pair with the jacket. While you probably won't find the exact fabric from which the suit is constructed, you can easily find a coordinate. If you want to keep the mono-chromatic look, search for a textured fabric in the same color as the jacket; the texture will bring in many slightly different shades of the color and the blend should look fantastic with your jacket.

- **Add a piece that is typically available in another season.** If you live in the northern hemisphere and are planning a ski trip to New Zealand in July (your summer), you may not be able to find the warm clothes you'll want for your trip. Since the fabric to make warm clothing is still readily available, once again the custom option can get you on your way in style.

- **To get exactly what you are envisioning.** Maybe it came to you in a dream—or you saw something like it in a movie—and now you just have to have that unforgettable dress. And wouldn't it be even better in periwinkle with a slightly fuller skirt? Well, you could search for your fantasy for the next several years and end up missing out, or you could call a custom dressmaker and get her to make the exact dress you are envisioning. Wow, you can be a designer without the years of study!

- **To ensure one-of-a-kind.** You've been invited to the Shindig of the Year. Wouldn't it be embarrassing to show up in the exact same dress as three other attendees? Once again, custom dressmaking comes to the rescue. With infinite styles, colors and fabrics from which to choose, a custom dress ensures that no one will be your evil twin on your big night. And even if the whole shindig thing is a big fantasy, why not be one-of-a-kind at your next birthday, cocktail or dinner party? What fun to have that power!

Enjoy Your Personalized Wardrobe

I hope you see now that building a capsule wardrobe based on ready-to-wear and custom-sewn or altered pieces is the best way to create the wardrobe of your dreams. Get started today and enjoy getting dressed every day!

JANA REZUCHA, AICI FLC
Real World Wardrobe

Look and feel great every day

(303) 413-1990
jana@realworldwardrobe.com
www.realworldwardrobe.com
www.mydiywardrobe.com

Real World Wardrobe creator Jana Rezucha believes that clothes are too often a distraction that drains people's energy.

Jana loves to show her clients how to easily, enjoyably and effortlessly get dressed every day. Her goal is to help her clients create wardrobes that feel so great that they can forget about their clothes and simply enjoy their lives, knowing they look their best.

Jana has often noticed that people straighten up or adjust their clothing when she mentions she is an image consultant. If you've been intimidated by the thought of hiring an image consultant, let Jana calm your fears and show you how satisfying and fun working with a wardrobe coach can be.

Jana's curious mind and love of learning has led her to a couple of degrees, several certificates and many, many courses in everything from microbiology to motorcycling and finance to fiber arts. Jana promises to apply all that she's learned to help you finally have a fun, functional, feel-great wardrobe that you love to wear—and forget!

Ordinary to Extraordinary: The Power of Accessories

Master the Art of Accessorizing for Your Body Type

By Nannette Bosh, CPC

Ever wonder why some women look completely pulled together right down to their jewels? Do you sometimes think to yourself, "How does she do that?" or "I wish I could pull that look off."? Well, you can. It is actually quite simple and most often done by using just the right accessories.

Have you ever skipped the accessories because you are not quite sure which accessory to pair with your outfit? Think of accessorizing your outfit like decorating or frosting a cake. Cakes come in many different sizes and shapes, as do women. Accessories—like cake decorations and frostings—are now available in a multitude of colors, styles, shapes and sizes. Embellishments abound and prices vary widely. Want to walk into a room and "take the cake"? You will become a real show-stopper with ease, gobbling up oodles of compliments by learning the basics of accessorizing for your body type. Even your ordinary, everyday outfit will be transformed into an extraordinary one!

Choosing the Right Necklace

Accessories, like clothing, will accentuate your best features.

As you may know, the V-neck is the most figure-flattering of all the shirt cuts. The depth of the V visually elongates the neckline, giving the appearance not only of a longer neck but of a thinner you. However, in my many years of experience, I have found that many women do not feel confident exposing a large amount of their chest area for whatever reason, especially as we age. In addition, most of us do not wish to share portions of our cupcakes, so to speak, with the entire office or the general public.

You certainly can wear your straight-line and scoop-neck tops—you simply need to create a "Virtual V" with your necklace. The longer the necklace, the deeper the V you will be able to create. To do this, you will want to select a necklace longer than 18 inches, and I generally recommend at least 21 inches. Remember, you are creating the illusion that you are wearing a deep V top, so your selection will not only need to lie flat in a V shape, but it will need to fall at or on the bustline. This is a perfect time to show off a pendant—they are great for holding beads or chains in the V position.

Do you love the extra-long beads and chain-style necklaces? I suggest you opt for layering it with a 21- to 25-inch piece. Necklaces that fall below the bustline or anywhere near the abdomen should not be worn alone; it is generally unflattering. This type of necklace will only create a virtual V if worn under the collar of a buttoned jacket.

Choosing the Right Earrings

Comfort and confidence should always come first.

Did you know that an overall softened, rounded chin is an attractive quality to the opposite sex because it is a sign of higher estrogen levels?

Earrings are a great way to soften the appearance of your face. If your face already has a soft appearance, don't worry—there is an earring for you, too.

If your face is long and square or your chin is slightly squared, you will want to select an earring that is fuller and perhaps rounded at the base. If you are dressing up for a night out on the town, you will want to grab the full, rounded chandeliers. Choosing an earring that has substance falling at the jawline actually fills out your face, creating a softer, more feminine appearance. If you happen to have a very round face and you are going out on the town, reach for the long and straight sparkle drops. In the daytime, the same rules apply, but you can tone down some of the sparkle.

If your neck is short like mine, you may want to opt for a sparkling stud on the lobe or a small, thin, front-facing crystal hoop. A longer earring on a shorter neck will make your neck seem shorter than it actually is.

Women with long hair are often faced with the disappearing earring dilemma. However, all of the above shape and size rules still apply. Needing your earring to show up with your longer hair is a situation that requires the use of color, not shape.

I always have a client try two different styles of earrings at the same time, one on each ear. Ninety-nine percent of the time, she prefers the one that feminizes her face, even though she has no idea why she chose it. Don't believe it? Please take a moment to go to the mirror and try it yourself with two different earring styles. To be certain you are comparing apples to apples, you'll be best served using earrings of the same shade or tone. When you see the actual effect of earring shape on your face, it will forever change how you shop for them in the future.

Choosing the Right Bracelet

Now you know it was meant for you, so wear it like you mean it.

Statement bracelets may be all the rage today and that is wonderful. However, if you have a delicate or dainty wrist, a statement bracelet can wind up leaving your arm looking a bit like a sausage and I am certain that is not something you would want. If your wrist is thin, stack several thin bracelets or bangles. If your wrist is wide, you may choose to be a statement bracelet wearer.

Always remember that your statement bracelet should hit you right on the bend of the wrist. Tubular forearms and wide wrists benefit from wide statement bracelets, because they create the illusion of a smaller wrist, thus making the arm appear more delicate. It's time to head back to the mirror, only this time you'll need to go to your full-length mirror. As with the earring example, you will want to try two different bracelets from the same color family. These tests really work best when you are viewing the same color or tone because it allows your eye to focus on size and cut instead of color. On one arm, place a wide statement bracelet at the bend of the wrist and on the other, try a bangle or a thin stretch bracelet. Which do you like better? Continue to wear the one you like best, and trade out your least favorite for a medium width. Still like your first choice? Well then, my friend, you have found your "it"-size bracelet.

When all is said and done, you will have determined which size and style bracelet is best to accentuate your wrist area. When you shop in the future, this will be your "go to" size each time you are selecting bracelets, regardless of color or embellishments.

Choosing the Right Bag

Bag trends come and go. Select the one that meets your needs.

Bags come in many different sizes and shapes. While a handbag serves the main function of holding all the things we women need in our busy daily lives, you do need to be careful that your handbag is not overloaded with everything but the kitchen sink. Just as small bags are lost on tall or larger women, shorter or smaller women can get lost in a too-large bag. If you find your body being swallowed by your bag, you may want to invest in a separate tote for all your non-essentials. Using an additional tote allows you to carry the handbag that complements you best. While traveling or at the office, you can put your smaller handbag right inside the tote.

It's not important whether you prefer an over-the-shoulder or an on-the-wrist carry, nor does it matter if you like one strap or two. It is my professional opinion that what matters most is the handbag size. I usually recommend carrying a bag that matches your stature. If you are short, try to lean toward a small or mid-size bag. If you are five feet, five inches or taller, mid-size to large handbags are fine. Are you the lucky woman who is almost six feet or taller? If so, go for the extra-large handbags. You could probably even get away with an all-out tote as your day bag.

There is one other thing to consider when you are selecting your bag of the day: does your weight fluctuate? Just between us girls, I am quite the foodie. If your weight fluctuates as mine does, then you may go through phases of having a great waistline to almost no waist at all. If so, you will need to change your bag shape accordingly. When my waist size increases, I opt for the horizontal rectangle-shaped bags, a style that allows me to visually cut my waist in half, giving the illusion I still have a waist.

Rings and Things

Anything goes today, so don't be afraid to mix it up.

I encourage you to try and break the habit—should you have it—of reaching for the same strand of pearls or gold chain day after day. We are going for extraordinary here, so dare to step outside the box. There are so many accessories! You don't need to wear them all at once, and you can wear as many as you are comfortable in. I would like to offer you a few pointers on some of the "extra" accessories. What about your rings, scarves, belts and jackets? That's right, in my opinion, even your jacket is actually an accessory, because it can be used in the exact same way we use all of our other accessories.

Are your fingers long or short? Fingers are like arms, so choosing ring size and shapes will be similar to choosing the right bracelet. If your fingers are long, feel free to wear a huge ring in almost any shape. If your fingers are short, there is still a decorative ring for you. However, short fingers can be a bit tricky, so you may want to stick to smaller band widths and rings that are in the diamond solitaire style, not allowing the top portion of the ring to pass the lowest wrinkle of your knuckle.

The short and sweet rule for scarves is simple; the longer your neck, the more bulk you can take from a scarf, but if you have a shorter neck, you may want to opt for a thinner scarf with a low knot. If you have a very short neck, use a thinner scarf under the lapels of your jacket.

Belts can help define a waist when worn over your top if you are wearing a pant without a bulky front. You will want to wear your belt on the small part of your waist. The best belt investment you can make is one that is more of a decorative jewelry style so you have lots of room for size adjustment. It will come in handy when layering your belt over a variety of thicknesses.

Last but not least is the jacket. Short woman—shorter jacket, tall woman—longer jacket is the general rule of thumb. No matter what jacket you select, the ultimate goal is to choose a jacket that has a taper right at your waistline. No taper? Then it is time to head to the tailor.

Getting a Handle on Color

It is important to find your personal style and then own it!

Most of us have learned at some point throughout the years which season of color suits us best, and we house a plethora of those colors in our closets. And of course we have a sprinkle of our own favorite shade, even if it didn't hit our seasonal color chart. At this point, let's talk about accessory color. As with clothing, the tone of your skin and color of your hair are used for your gold and silver indicators. Gold shows best with tan, brown and dark skin tones; light and fair skin tones often do best with silver. Whatever your preference, the choice is now yours because it is finally perfectly acceptable to mix the two. What about other colors and multiple colors in the same accessory piece? Also perfectly acceptable, and they provide a lot of flexibility when you're combining pieces.

After all the years I have been in the fashion accessory business, I have one of the best-kept secrets that I will now share with you. This secret, I assure you, will forever change the way you get dressed. Take some time to organize your clothes and accessory items by type first, then by color. It may take a little time, but it will be worth every second. My own closet is organized this way, and when I am selecting my outfit, I first grab the accessories that fit my mood, and then I build my outfit around my accessories. That's it, the secret is out of the bag.

Let's say you're in a "jeans, jacket and scoop-neck T-shirt mood." What will you need? Well, if you plan to wear your jacket buttoned, you can, as I mentioned earlier, go with the extra-long beads or chain-style necklace for under the collar of your jacket. However, if you are wearing the jacket open, as I often do, then grab one of your favorite multi-colored necklaces that will hold a virtual V shape. Glide it across your different shades of jeans. See a great match? Then those are your jeans for today. Pull the jeans off the clothes pole and with the necklace and jeans in hand, do the same "glide" to the jackets in your closet. When you find the jacket that goes with both of these pieces, pull out the jacket. Then take all of these pieces and head over to your T-shirts to select the color that goes best with all of your previously-selected pieces.

Missing something? Yes, you most certainly are. After you are completely dressed and wearing your necklace, you will then select your shoes and handbag or purse. It is at this point you will be able to see if there is any additional color or colors from the necklace of the day that you would like to add to your outfit as an additional accent. That is why we love all of our shoes and can't part with any of our handbags. Choose your favorite gold or silver earrings, throw on a couple of your matching "it" bracelets and bam! You're done. Now you are in your ordinary jeans and you look extraordinary—so head out to the supermarket or on an errand and grab yourself some compliments. As the compliments pour in, you will feel your self-esteem climb, *and that, my dear girl, is the power of accessories!*

NANNETTE BOSH, CPC
Bangle and Clutch

Accessories and tips for a life that kicks!

(860) 896-1208
nannette@bangleandclutch.com
www.bangleandclutch.com

A keen eye for spotting up-and-coming style trends, having been featured countless times in print and televised media—including a CBS Primetime Special—and 10 years of fashion industry experience make Nannette an accessory expert. After longing for a career that would benefit women and feed her passion for fashion, she now has it! A sought-after style consultant, Certified Lifestyle Coach and speaker, Nannette assists many women—including some celebrities—seeking a style of their own. She also guides them through their journey of self-discovery. Feeling beautiful is life's best accessory, and in order to feel truly beautiful, women need to be able to communicate their wants and needs effectively.

A social media maverick, Nannette holds three of the top Twitter fashion industry accounts and reaches an Internet audience of more than 120,000. She also offers exposure for those looking to jump-start their social media. Once a single mother and nearly broke, Nannette enthusiastically helps women looking to unlock their true potential, taking great pride in supporting female-focused charities as well as her clients.

Clean Your Closet to Shop Your Closet
Less Is Always More

By Cynthia Postula, MA, AICI FLC

A coworker told me a story some years back that I've never forgotten. He gave, in great detail, a long description of a shiatsu massage he had barely endured over the weekend. With a contorted facial expression, he spoke about what an ordeal it had been. The massage was actually painful. I couldn't help asking why he chose to put himself through— let alone pay for—such a grueling experience. He replied, "Because it feels so good when it's over."

Many women look at the task of cleaning out their closet as overwhelming, grueling, and even painful—well, at least emotionally. They don't know where to begin, and feel paralyzed about making so many decisions about which clothes to keep and which ones to expel from their lives forever. I am here to tell you that if you can summon up the courage to face this task, you will reap wondrous rewards. Relief is the first one, followed by satisfaction so sweet as to put a big smile on your face. Why? Because after your closet clean-out, you will dress with ease, pleasure and confidence. As one client put it recently, "Oh my God, what a great sense of relief I had when I finished. It is so great to walk into my closet and see exactly what I have, what I love and what fits me now. I feel lighter. I get dressed quickly and I look good. It is just so much less stressful!"

Do You Really Need All That?

Closet cleaning is made complicated for many women because we have accumulated so much stuff, and our walk-in closets hold more clothes than we will ever need—or can even find. *Most women in this country wear only 20 percent of their clothing 80 percent of the time.* We can learn so much from our European sisters. These stylish women generally have small armoires in which they store a few key, well-made, quality garments that mix and match well together. Their philosophy is "less is more." They spend their money on a limited number of basic, classic, simple neutrals (black/gray, white/cream, navy, camel/brown), and then add accessories (the beloved scarf for example, or a long strand of knotted pearls) to create great style, even pizzazz. Coco Chanel herself often suggested that women own a few quality, well-chosen pieces that allow them to dress with ease and elegance.

Having a lot of clothes does not translate into making a lot of coordinated outfits. In fact, it often leaves us confused and indecisive. It can be like trying to create a meal from numerous disparate ingredients. Think, however, of how many culinary creations can be made from *basic* ingredients like flour, butter, eggs, milk and sugar. With small quantities of spices, "accessories" if you will, you can vary the mix and make enough different cakes to fill a cookbook. When you stick with the basics, life gets instantly simpler and more satisfying. Cake is *always* simply satisfying, right?

Over the last few years, partly because of the economy, there have been several movements afoot to pare down and simplify everything, including our closets. The *New York Times* recently had a feature story about a small group of women who decided to stop buying more clothes, and to wear only six clothing items for one month. They called it a "shopping diet." Many of the "Sixers" gave up after a couple of weeks, probably due to the boredom of wearing so few—usually black—pieces. That story reminds me of the nuns in my Catholic school who wore black and white habits every single day for years. Of course, they were dedicated to poverty, chastity and obedience. But we are not nuns. Besides, not all of us look good in black and white. We want to have fun with fashion. Women love to express themselves by wearing appealing clothing that promotes feelings of competence, confidence, romance, creativity or playfulness.

Let's not get carried away with these extremes—having either too much or too little. I am not suggesting doing major closet surgery. Let's just take a reasonable, responsible look at the clothing in your closet. You can decide what you honestly need that works for your body type, coloring and current lifestyle, and you will discover what you should purge. This process will eliminate confusion and indecisiveness when you stand in front of your closet every single day asking that age-old question, *"What am I going to wear?"*

So let's get started. I suggest you divide the time into short segments and conquer accordingly. Set a timer and work for only 60 minutes. Then stop for awhile or for the day.

Out with the Old

In that first hour, clear out anything from the closet that is not related to dressing:

- Find a new home for the photo albums, craft supplies and yoga mats.
- Remove formal wear, special occasion or travel garments (gowns, heavy jackets and coats, ski pants) and put them in another closet.

- Remove faded, old items that you have not worn for three or more years.
- Remove clothes you do not enjoy wearing or that make you feel sloppy or uncomfortable. Be honest!
- Group all athletic and exercise wear separately.
- Take all jeans off hangers, fold them, and put them on a shelf.

Now your closet will be more open and roomy, with fewer garments —the ones you are wearing consistently. It is important to check again for any clothing item that does not make you feel upbeat, competent, polished, confident and comfortable. Let's talk about comfort and ease. It does not mean oversized and sloppy. Almost every client with whom I have worked has a number of too-large, old, inexpensive sweatshirts, sweat suits, or baggy T-shirts and pants that are "just for wearing around the house." I believe that you can be cozy and comfortable in clothing that flatters, fits and feels good. Why not let your family, the most important people in your life, see you looking relaxed *and* attractive?

I tell my clients to buy the best quality they can afford for every occasion. However I could not argue with one woman who lived on a farm and needed some old, worn clothes to "de-worm the goats!" Quality fabrics always wash better, wear longer, drape better and feel great on your skin. Think of natural materials like cotton, silk, light wool, linen, and my all-time favorite, cashmere. Remember, the clothing we wear affects how we feel and how others see us.

Back to the task at hand.

Group and Try On

Next, hang all your jackets together, separating them from the skirts or pants they came with. Then group all tops together, pants together, skirts and dresses together.

Label four large garbage bags or boxes with the words *Donate, Clean/Repair, Consign* and *Don't Know.* In this last bag you will place items that you are not sure about, such as something that is sentimental, or that you like but have not been wearing for whatever reason. *Decide quickly, don't analyze.*

If your timer goes off, stop and think if you want to continue. If so, set the timer for the next desired amount of time. Take another deep breath.

Now you must try on each of your jackets. Have a full-length mirror so you can see how they fit your figure now, from the front and the back. Ask these four questions:

1. Does this really fit me?
2. Is it flattering to my body shape and coloring?
3. Do I love wearing it?
4. Is it in style?

If the answer to all four questions is an honest yes, place the jacket back in the closet. If the answer is no to *any* of the questions, place in the appropriate box/bag. Do not keep anything that is more than two sizes off.

About jackets: They are a key wardrobe piece to add impact, color and warmth. They add instant authority in the workplace. Each one should coordinate with several bottom pieces. For today's style, think about shortening a jacket that is too long, especially if you are petite (under five feet, five inches tall).

Check your timer now and stop if you need to.

When you return to the task, ask the same four questions as you try on each of your tops, pants (including the folded jeans), dresses and skirts. Put each article back in the closet or in one of the designated bags/boxes.

Accessories are what make outfits creative and fun. If you cannot see your accessories because they are in drawers, baskets, or otherwise out of sight, bring them into the light now. *If you do not see it, you will not remember to wear it.* Take a cursory look at all scarves, belts, jewelry and shoes, and eliminate anything that is old, worn or uncomfortable (as in shoes). Find the appropriate box/bag to put it in. Otherwise, keep the good stuff in sight. Accessories are the frosting on the cake and add deliciousness to any outfit.

Congratulations! You are well on your way to an organized, simplified, wearable closet. We are coming to the best, most exciting and fun part. We are going to coordinate and actually shop the very closet you just cleaned.

Down to Basics

First we should review what the experts—and probably the French— think are the essential wardrobe basics. You might consider paring down your cleaned closet even further:

- Jackets in neutral colors (3 neutrals, 1 denim, 1 evening)
- Blouses/tops in neutrals (3) and striped/colored shirts, camisoles/tees
- Sweater set (1)
- Jeans (1 dark-wash dressy, 1 casual)
- Pants in neutral colors, unembellished (3)
- Skirts in solid, neutral colors, A-line or pencil (3)
- Dresses (1 LBD or another solid neutral, 1 print)
- Shoes (a flat, a loafer, a sandal, black/brown pumps, boots, athletic shoes, dressy evening shoes)
- Handbags (a tote, a shoulder bag, an evening clutch)
- Scarves for color, warmth and those that bring attention to the face
- Belts in leather for day and fabric for evening
- Jewelry (watch for day/evening, pearls, diamonds, metallics)
- Outerwear (trench/jacket/sweater and winter coat in neutral colors)

Note: I keep mentioning neutral colors, as they are so important in every closet. Do you really know which ones are your best shades? Black and white can be go-to colors for some women, while on others, they are much too harsh. Having a color analysis is essential to knowing for certain which colors most flatter your skin tone, hair and eye colors. Color analysis is more exact and sophisticated than it was in the 1970s. Many image consultants offer this service, and you will never have to guess at your colors again. For more about color analysis, see Dawn Stebbing's chapter, *Enhance Your Image with Color,* on page 49.

Let's Go Shopping in Your Closet!

Have paper and pen handy to fill in a wardrobe chart, like the one below. You will need several copies. Or use a digital camera to photograph every outfit you put together.

Wardrobe Coordination					
Jacket	Pant/Skirt	Dress	Blouse/ Sweater	Accessory	What to Shop For
Ralph Lauren Navy Blazer	DKNY Cream Pant		RL Cream Silk Blouse	Spect. Pumps Navy/Red Scarf	Cream Belt

- Take the first jacket hanging in the closet and lay it on your bed. Take out each of your tops/pants/skirts in the closet, hold it near the jacket and ask yourself, "Can these be worn together?" If yes, then add your accessories (belt, scarf, shoes and jewelry) to complete each outfit. If the jacket does not coordinate with anything, consider eliminating it. Then go on to the next jacket and continue this process. My clients are invariably surprised and delighted by seeing all the new combinations they never noticed before.

- Fill in the wardrobe chart with special outfits you want to remember, or photograph each completed outfit. Notice the last column marked "Shop For" and fill that in with whatever is needed to finish an outfit. If that need repeats, it will be a key item to place on your shopping list.

Whew! This can be exhausting and energizing at the same time. Hang in there.

- After going through all your jackets, repeat this process with each of your other categories of clothing, including your skirts, tops and dresses. Then fill in the wardrobe chart with these new combinations.

- Place all clothing back in your closet in their various categories, and arrange each section from lighter to darker colors.

- Return all shoes, belts, jewelry and scarves to a shelf or section where they are now *visible.*

Putting It Back in Style

If your clothing is lined up on old, mismatched hangers, now is the time to count the pieces you have, then shop for some pretty matching hangers, as well as for belt, scarf and jewelry holders. Particularly helpful is the style of hanging jewelry holder that has forty clear pockets on each side of it. You can see all your items at a glance, and it hangs alongside your clothing. Two great sources for these are Bed Bath & Beyond®, and The Container Store®. Also, if your closet is small and does not have shelving, think about moving a bookcase into the closet or having shelves built in along a wall. Check out Pottery Barn®, Crate & Barrel®, or Pier 1® for pretty baskets or clear shoe boxes or storage bins. Just remember to keep things within view.

The more we use something, the more important it is to us, and the more we want to maintain it. Make sure that alterations are done promptly, that shoes are in good repair, and that garments are always clean and fresh. Steaming is easier than ironing. Rowenta® makes a great little hand-held steamer for loosening wrinkles on garments for just $50. You want your clothes to be "standing at the ready" so you can dress with ease and pleasure at all times.

Whenever you buy something new for your wardrobe, give away an older article to someone who will appreciate it. That way, you will keep your closet from getting too full all over again.

The Reward

Now stand in front of your closet and take it all in. What do you see? I know you see clothes you enjoy, that fit you now, and that are fun and stylish. They are all in such good order and ready to wear in all kinds of new combinations! Can you stand it?

You have worked hard. Your body is achy and tired. Now may be the perfect time to reward yourself with a massage. Perhaps you have experienced enough pain for awhile, and want to forego anything with the word "shiatsu" in it. Maybe a soothing Swedish massage is just the ticket to comfort and relax you after a job well done.

CYNTHIA POSTULA, MA, AICI FLC
Look Great, Feel Great Image Consulting

(561) 371-7187
cynthia@lookgreatfeelgreatic.com
www.lookgreatfeelgreatic.com

Cynthia Postula is a certified image consultant who is passionate about helping women and men look great and feel great about themselves. With a master's degree in clinical psychology, her first career was in the counseling field, where she advised and mediated issues in the workplace as an Employee Assistance Program Manager.

Upon leaving the corporate world in 1996, Cynthia completed extensive training in all aspects of fashion and image consulting for men and women at Color One Associates in Washington, D.C.

Besides working with men and women individually on style, proportion, colors, makeup, accessorizing and etiquette, Cynthia designed and teaches 10 fashion classes at a number of venues.

A particular passion of hers is to help people in transition who have lost—or never found—their own unique style, and who are ready to focus on making the most of their appearance. As a result of their work with Cynthia, they not only look great, they feel increased confidence, well-being and success in their professional and personal lives.

Wake Up Your Makeup

Your Hands-On Guide to the Power of Makeup

By Brenda Azevedo

Did you know that an assumption about you is made within the first few seconds of seeing you? You have not spoken a word. In addition, according to countless studies, it is hard to ever change that first impression. We communicate many things in those first 10 seconds that could affect our personal and professional life. Advancing in our jobs, our income and ultimately our happiness can all teeter on someone else's perception of us. "We make an assumption about someone within 10 seconds of being introduced, this impression is largely based on his or her looks—and doesn't change very easily," says Oregon State social psychologist Frank Bernieri, PhD, in the November 2009 issue of *Cosmopolitan* magazine.

What role can makeup play in your first impression? As it turns out, makeup can enhance your looks and help you feel more confident and more powerful. Others will perceive you as healthier, cleaner and much more successful. When you are comfortable in your own skin, you feel better about yourself and you are able to take on the world in a powerful way.

"I had no idea of the character. But the moment I was dressed, the clothes and the makeup made me feel the person he was. I began to know him, and by the time I walked onto the stage he was fully born."
—Charlie Chaplin, English comic actor and film director

Only Fix the Mistakes

I recently attended a class in which the instructor said over and over, "Only fix mistakes, not the content of your project." Wow, that statement really hit me. What I see in my makeup studio every day are women who take the power of makeup and use it against themselves. What do I mean by that? These women want to change the content—*their natural beauty*—and not just fix the mistakes—*their perceived imperfections.*

We know that enhancing ourselves with makeup can help us be perceived in a better light. Too much makeup—used to *mask* the real you—can be damaging to that perception. Makeup should enhance you, express the real you to the world. Good makeup sharpens the focus and can allow you to naturally feel better about yourself.

Obtaining this makeup balance can overwhelm the busy woman. Often it is easier to just follow the old makeup routine we have used since high school. Natural beauty is a far cry from the kind of makeup I was applying in high school. How about you? It is easy to add to the problem by just doing more of what we learned in the past in an attempt to get our look just right. The issue is *how* to use our makeup, to be the boss of our makeup once and for all.

Makeup can define your facial features. Makeup can distract attention away from imperfections. Makeup can give you a smooth, youthful appearance. What makeup cannot do is apply itself.

Highlight Your Best Features

"Mirror, Mirror, on the wall,
show me my best features—I can't see them at all."
—Someone who doesn't believe she is fairest of them all

Before you can express and highlight your best features, you must honestly know what they are. The truth is that our brain is more powerful than our eyes. After years in the beauty business, one thing I am sure of is that we do not really *see* ourselves. We look in the mirror every day; however, we fail to *see* our own natural beauty. Actually, many of us are uncomfortable with our natural beauty. I venture to guess that you might be cringing right now, thinking you have *no* natural beauty. Are you stuck in that belief? When you try on a new look, do you feel "this is not me" or "I cannot reproduce this look every day"? Time and again I see women who have handed over their beauty power to one feature of their face that they see as flawed. They spend all their energy focusing on or attempting to mask that feature, ignoring their beauty as a whole. Allowing your brain to get comfortable with your natural look is the first key to using your makeup well.

To arrive anywhere we need a map. You would not follow a map that would take you to Florida when your destination was Hawaii, would you? Well, your face map is the same. You need to follow your own course to get to the perfect reflection of you. What is your face shape? What is your eye shape? Do you have dark circles under your eyes or redness in your skin? The first powerful step is to identify your features and issues. What do you want to highlight? What do you want to minimize? Let us begin.

Choosing a Foundation

Foundation is one of the biggest reasons I became a custom cosmetic blender. The true *foundation* of makeup *is* the foundation. A smooth, clear, youthful complexion is a universal desire. So it makes sense that the most important makeup choice you make is a foundation. If you choose a foundation that does not match your skin tone, everything else you put on your face will be less than flattering. If you want to have a little more color in your skin, always choose to do that with a bronzer, not with your foundation. Keeping your foundation color true to you will always be more youthful and flattering.

The texture of your skin must be considered when choosing the perfect foundation. Many companies offer oil-free, enriched or matte formulas. Mineral powders or tinted moisturizers are also an option. The key is to try the foundation on and let it settle on the skin for a few moments. Then check it in good lighting. You want to make sure it blends into your skin.

Covering Up

Concealer is a woman's best-kept secret to appearing refreshed when she is not! Choose a concealer that is one shade lighter than your foundation. For dark circles, apply the concealer in the inside corner of the eye. Blend outward, feathering with a synthetic brush until the concealer blends seamlessly into your skin. As you are blending the concealer, it will be concentrated in the inner part of the eye area and will fade as you get out to the *crow's feet* area at the outside of our eye. You don't want to accentuate the fine lines.

Most concealers are oil- or cream-based to allow for hydration and a smooth, silky finish. One warning about concealer: it is a product that will need to be *set* with a mineral or translucent powder to keep it from moving to another place on your face.

Eye Makeup for All Eye Shapes

The almond shape. This eye shape is so named because it literally has an almond shape and is upswept at the outer corner. Use the following steps to help almond eyes appear larger and rounded:

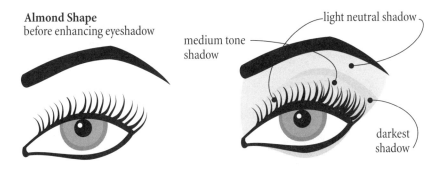

1. Cover the entire lid, from your lash line to your brow line, with a light, neutral eye shadow.

2. At the crease line, apply medium-toned eye shadow; blend up toward the brow bone. Be sure to keep the color in the center of the eye area.

3. Apply your darker eye shadow on the outer third or corner of the eyelid, making an arrow shape with the eye shadow color. Then blend inward and upward.

4. Eyeliner on the upper lid can make almond eyes appear large. To have your almond eyes look more round, make the liner slightly thicker at the middle of the eye and stop eyeliner before the outer corner of the eye.

5. Shadow smudged on the lower lash line in the center of the lower lid will round off the look.

Close-set eyes. If the space between your eyes is shorter than the width of one eye, you have close-set eyes. With this eye shape, we want to create space with the illusion of width between the eyes.

Close-set eyes
before enhancing eyeshadow

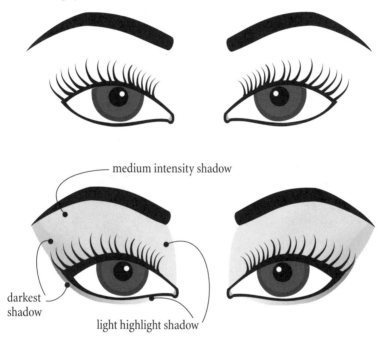

medium intensity shadow

darkest
shadow

light highlight shadow

1. Apply a light highlight color from the inside corner of the eye up to the brow bone.

2. Apply a medium-intensity eye shadow to the outer corner of your eye, from lash line up to the brow bone, and blend well.

3. Add a rich, dark color of eye shadow to the lash line, sweeping to the outer corner.

4. Line the eye. The liner should begin over the iris area of the eye and sweep out, extending beyond the end of the eye to maximize the lengthening effect. Keep the color concentrated toward the outside corners of the eye.

5. Smudge the darkest eye shadow shade onto the lower lash line from the iris line and out, keeping the inside area of the eye clear of the dark shadow.

6. Apply your highlight shadow color to the lower lash area from your tear duct area; sweep out to meet the dark shadow (the area that you kept clear of color in step 5.)

7. Mascara should be concentrated on the outer area of the eye. For a special effect, artificial lashes can be applied to the outside corners of the eye. That will make the eyes appear further apart.

8. Your brows should be tweezed slightly further out from the nose area to add space and create a more balanced look.

Wide-set eyes. If the space between your eyes is greater than the width of one eye, you have wide-set eyes. Our goal is to make the eyes appear closer by eliminating some space, just the opposite of the close–set eye.

Wide-set eyes
before enhancing eyeshadow

light highlight shadow

darkest shadow

1. To minimize or reduce the space between the eyes, apply a dark eye shadow to the inner corner of the eyelid. Start your dark color in the tear duct area and extend it upward toward the brow bone and outward to the first one-third of the lid.

2. Next, apply your lighter eye shadow to the outer two-thirds of the lid; blend upward to the brow bone.

3. Apply eyeliner to the entire eye. For a softer liner effect, you can use a dark eye shadow.

4. Mascara should be applied to the inner corner of the eye and out. If you want to apply artificial lashes, use a full strip or apply individual lashes to the entire eye.

5. Your brows should be filled in closer to your nose to eliminate space and visually pull the eyes closer.

The hooded eye. I like to call this a *bedroom eye*. Many of my clients who have this eye shape are frustrated because the eye appears to be partially closed. With this eye shape, the upper lid covers the lash line. Many women feel that they cannot wear shadow on this eye shape. We can—all we need to do is create a crease.

Hooded Eye
before enhancing eyeshadow

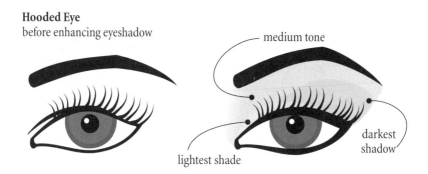

medium tone

darkest shadow

lightest shade

1. Use a light highlight shade from the lash line up to the brow bone.

2. Apply a shade slightly darker than the highlight shade over the outer third of the lid and extend up to the area where you want to create a

crease or indentation on the eyelid. You can find this area by pressing gently at the top of the eye socket area and feeling where it naturally indents.

3. Use a darker contour shade on the outer corner, sweeping up and inward. Use a windshield wiper motion to blend that darker shade in to create a crease.

4. It is important to use a liner to define the lash line of this eye shape.

The prominent eye. For this shape, we want to help reduce the appearance of the eye and help make the eye appear as if it is receding rather than bulging.

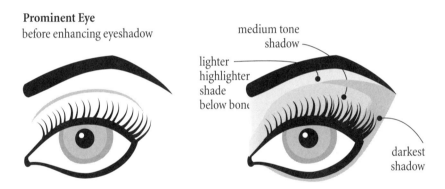

Prominent Eye
before enhancing eyeshadow

medium tone
shadow

lighter
highlighter
shade
below bone

darkest
shadow

1. Use a medium eye shadow shade and apply to the entire eyelid from lash line to brow bone.

2. Start at the lash line with a slightly darker eye shadow shade and blend up toward the brow bone. Concentrate the darkest color near the lash line.

3. Apply the darkest color in the outer corner of the eye in an inverted arrow pattern.

4. Stroke a lighter highlighter shade under the brow bone and blend well.

5. Line the lash line with a soft, wider smudge of color, adding depth instead of a hard line.

6. Line your lower lashes.

Beautiful Brows

Brows are so important to your overall look. They communicate so much and really accentuate your look. Brows can give you an immediate eye lift. You can look younger and polished when your brows are groomed and cared for.

I am asked daily:

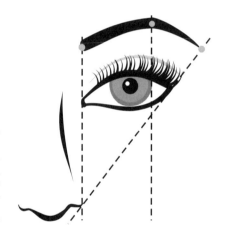

- Where should my brows begin?

- How much of an arch do I need?

- Where should my brows end?

Here is a simple exercise to help you find the answers. Grab an eyeliner pencil and a regular long pencil or a straw. Line the pencil or straw straight up, starting at your tear duct area, extending it into your brow area. Put a dot where it lines up with your brow line. Does your actual brow start there?

Next, the high point of your arch should be above the outer edge of your iris. Add a dot there. Take the pencil or straw and lay it from the outer nostril diagonally to the corner of your eye and into your brow area. Put your final dot there.

Step back and look at your result. Do the dots line up to where your brows are? Close? If you have brow hairs that extend beyond the dots, you can remove a few to attain a natural shape. If, on the other hand, your brows are sparse, you can fill in the missing hairs with a pencil or some eyebrow powder.

There are several tools on the market to help you achieve and maintain the perfect brow shape. Stencils are a great way to try on different brow looks. Choose a stencil that is in proportion to the structure of your face. Most stencil sets have a few different shapes that you can try on. Choose the one that opens up your face.

Decorating with Blush and Lipstick

Although blush is one of the last steps in your makeup application, don't underestimate its importance. Blush adds a fresh, healthy glow.

It is best if you choose a blush color that mimics how your skin would normally flush, say after a nice run or workout. To apply your blush, choose a fluffy blush brush, then smile at yourself in the mirror. Apply your blush on the high spot of the apples of your cheeks. Blend the color, softening any hard edges.

Want the perfect lipstick shade? The easiest way to find your perfect shade is to pull out your bottom lip. Based on the natural color you see there, choose a lipstick color one to two shades deeper than that. Beware of choosing too deep a shade; deep lipstick colors can be harsh and can age you. The softer the lip color, the fuller the lips appear. Lips make a powerful impression. If you only have time to use one makeup product, I would say make it your lip color. Indeed, lipstick *is* the fire that lights the face.

Finding Your Makeup Personality

I encourage you to experiment and find your own makeup personality.

- Express *your* sense of self; it is not about conforming to someone else's style of beauty.

- Bring your unique features to life and you will feel confident and, yes, powerful.

- Toss out some of the old beauty rules you learned years ago and explore, experiment and have fun with makeup.

- Decide what you want your first impression to be and apply your makeup accordingly.

If you feel good about how you look, others will see you in a positive light. Remember—the first and most important key to your transformation with makeup is to look in the mirror with a bare face and love what has always been there.

BRENDA AZEVEDO
just B Cosmetics

Makeup created with a style all your own

(916) 879-3006
brenda@justbcosmetics.com
www.justbcosmetics.com

Brenda, a professional freelance makeup artist, is the founder and owner of just B Cosmetics, a custom-blending makeup bar and gift boutique located in Sacramento, California.

Having been in the beauty business since 1983, and as the former owner of an award-winning day spa in Carmichael, she shares her significant hands-on experience with her clients. Brenda brings this expertise to you to help positively impact how you feel about yourself!

Brenda's specialty is matching women with the perfect foundation shade and customizing the formula for the individual's unique skin type. Her beauty philosophy is "Be one in a million, not one of a million."

Brenda is passionate about teaching and sharing this makeup philosophy and developing the tools women need to do this with ease. She conducts beauty workshops around the country, and mentors with other makeup artists. Brenda has been featured as a beauty consultant on BlogTalkRadio's *The Fitness IQ* and has been the recipient of the "Best Makeup" award by KCRA's A List two years in a row.

Hairstyles of Distinction

By Ronda Anderson, MA, AICI FLC

Have you ever heard the saying, "Your hair is your crowning glory"? Just as your clothing styles reflect who you are and your personality, likewise, your hairstyle is an indication of your personal fashion style and taste. Your hair is an essential part of your image and one of the first things others notice.

In this chapter, you will gain a better understanding of how to choose:

- The right hairstyle for you
- The right hair color
- When it is time for a haircut versus a trim
- Hair alternatives
- A hairstylist that is right for you

Before we move forward, here is a hairstyle assessment to help you evaluate your own hairstyle.

Hairstyle Assessment	Yes	No
1. Do you change or update your hairstyle at least once a year?		
2. Do you use hair color or highlights to enhance your natural hair color?		
3. Does your hairstyle enhance your facial shape?		
4. Does your hairstyle enhance your body proportions?		
5. Does your hairstyle reflect your career objectives?		

If you answered no to one or more of these five questions, then it is time for you to update your hairstyle.

Choosing the Right Hairstyle

Your hair plays an important part in what your image communicates to others. As women, we have the awesome privilege to express our various moods, personality and unique style with our hair. We can wig it, weave it, color it, cut it, braid it, twist it, flip it, curl it and straighten it. You name it and we will find a way to tame even the unruliest of hair and use it to express how we feel about ourselves.

Every woman has her own signature hairstyle that may set a trend for others to follow. In the 1970s, the late Farrah Fawcett made the feathered bangs style look fabulous. Every woman during those years copied her signature look. In 2002, Halle Berry gave a new meaning to short and sassy. Her short, pixie hairstyle was always picture perfect and she received a lot of attention.

Finding the right hairstyle is like finding the right shoe—you check out the latest trends and select the right fit, length and colors that are suitable for your personality and lifestyle. Every hairstyle and hair color that is right for your friend, colleague, family member or favorite celebrity may not be right for you.

This is why it is important to seek professional advice about which hairstyles will look best on you and will correspond to your fashion personality.

According to Frieda Perry, who has 18 years of experience as a hairstylist and is the owner of Frieda's Hair Salon in Rex, Georgia, one of the biggest mistakes women make with their hair is applying chemicals—colors, relaxers and the like—themselves. Frieda further states, "The major part of the hair care industry is the correction of chemical damage and bad color."

To avoid these types of mistakes, we recommend that you consult with a professional hairstylist who can analyze your hair and provide you with the treatment that will result in healthy hair.

You and Your Hairstyle Personality

Why is choosing the right hairstyle important? Your hairstyle is a reflection of your fashion personality. When you have a better understanding of your fashion personality, you will know how to coordinate your hairstyle to reflect your clothing style. There are at least four basic hairstyle personalities: Classic, Natural, Romantic and Dramatic.

Classic styles. If you wear the traditional two-piece business suit, then you might wear a hairstyle that exhibits sophistication and elegance.

Natural styles. If you like wearing outfits that are more relaxed and carefree, then your hairstyle may be free-flowing with layers, it may be cut short or you may wear braids. Whichever way you decide to wear your hair, it will always be low-maintenance.

Romantic styles. If you like to wear clothing styles with a romantic flair such as ruffles and lace, then your hairstyle may feature soft curls or waves.

Dramatic styles. If your outfits are characterized by a strong, bold or elaborate look, then your hair may be in an asymmetrical style or be cut in a blunt or angular bob.

A rule of thumb for coordinating your outfits with your hairstyle is to ask yourself the following questions:

1. Is my hairstyle fitting for the occasion?
2. Does my hairstyle reflect the image I would like to communicate?
3. Does my hairstyle correspond to the outfit I am wearing?

Criteria for Choosing Your Signature Hairstyle

There are many things to consider when you are choosing a new hairstyle. One of the first things your stylist will look at when helping you choose a hairstyle is your facial shape.

There are four basic facial shapes to consider: oval, round, square and heart.

Oval shape. With an oval facial shape, your face shape is well-balanced with even proportions. There are a variety of hairstyles that will look great on you. You can wear your hair in various lengths, from short or medium to long styles.

Oval

Round shape. If you have a round facial shape, your face has fullness around the chin and the hairline. With this facial shape, I suggest you wear hairstyles that are longer than your chin length and keep your haircut close to your face to help your face appear longer and narrower.

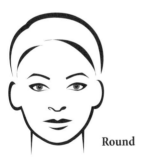

Round

Square shape. A square facial shape has a strong, square jawline. To soften the look of your jawline, wear layers around your face, with wispy bangs. I also suggest that you add height to your crown area to lengthen your facial shape.

Square

Heart Shape. This shape has features that are wide at the temples and hairline and narrow to a small, refined chin. Hairstyles that are chin-length or longer look best on the heart-shaped face. I recommend a chin-length bob for this facial shape because it gives a balanced appearance.

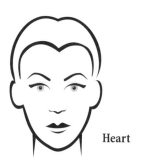

Heart

A second factor to consider when choosing a hairstyle is how your hair length fits your body proportions. I am sure you are wondering what your body proportions have to do with your hair. Before explaining what I mean by this, let me first remind you of a special character on the *Addams Family,* Cousin Itt.

If you recall the movie or the television show, Cousin Itt was very short, was covered with hair from head to toe, and always wore a hat. You never saw his eyes or his face. All you saw was hair in motion, running to and fro. When watching the sitcom, I always wondered what Cousin Itt looked like under all that hair. I am sure Cousin Itt would be any hairstylist's delight. Who would not want to take a pair of scissors to Cousin Itt's long, straight locks and keep cutting until you saw his face?

Similarly, when you see a woman with a petite body frame and excessively long hair that nearly covers her face, your first thought may be that she should pull her hair away from her face so you can see her facial features. Another issue with too much hair is that it may overpower your body proportions and make you appear larger or heavier than you really are.

Third, when choosing a hairstyle that is right for you, you should consider your career objectives. Ask yourself these two questions:

1. Does my hairstyle fit the position I currently have?
2. Does my hairstyle fit the future position that I would like to have?

Just as your clothing styles reflect your professional work environment, your hair should do the same. For example, if you work in a law office, more than likely your fashion style will be conservative to reflect the atmosphere of the office environment. You may wish to wear a more classic hairstyle to fit the tone of the office.

Wearing a hairstyle that conflicts with the dress code standards of your chosen career may tarnish your opportunities to be seen as a professional in your work environment.

Choosing the Right Hair Color

When choosing a hair color, one of the main factors to consider is your complexion. Will the color you have chosen enhance your complexion? Is it too intense, or does it wash you out?

Your hair color should not be so overpowering that it creates a harsh look. A good hairstylist will find the right color balance to brighten your complexion and make it glow. In fact, when you choose the right hair color, you can actually take years off your face.

To help your stylist make the right decisions about your hair color, ask yourself the following questions:

1. What do you want the hair color to do for you? For example, do you want it to highlight your hair or cover the gray?

2. Do you prefer permanent color or semi-permanent? Permanent color lasts longer through shampoos, whereas semi-permanent will last through six to eight shampoos.

3. How much are you willing to spend to maintain your hair color? Each type of hair coloring method may have a different price. You will have to decide what is within your budget and how much you want to spend on the coloring method.

When to Cut and When to Trim

Imagine this: You are looking through every hair magazine trying to find the right style for you. Your mind keeps telling you, "I need a fresh new look!" Meanwhile your insides are trembling, asking "What if I don't like it? What if it doesn't look right? What if my husband doesn't like it? What if my children laugh at it?" The "what ifs" go on and on until you talk yourself out of a new hairstyle again. Does this sound familiar?

What is the difference between a haircut and a trim? The difference is the need, desire and willingness for a transformation. Every woman comes to a point in her life when she needs and wants to be transformed. Some people call it reinventing yourself. When it happens, it is like a rebirth. You feel alive and your self-confidence is sky-high. Depending on your needs and desires, you may decide on a drastic transformation or a subtle one. A haircut is indicated when you need or desire a drastic transformation. Choose a trim when you want a subtle change. Regardless of whether you choose a cut or a trim, make sure you are comfortable with the changes and will be happy with the results.

To select the cut that is right for you, bring your hairstylist various pictures that you like of hairstyles in three lengths—short, medium and long. A good hairstylist will be able to adapt the hairstyle to your facial shape, your personality and your lifestyle. In this way, your stylist will be able to help you make the adjustments from a trim to a haircut without your feeling pressured or having any regrets.

Many women ask, "How often should I update my hairstyle?" Our expert, Frieda, recommends that you update your hairstyle at least once a year. It doesn't have to be drastic. You can make subtle changes to your hairstyle such as tweaking your hair color, changing the way you wear your bangs, or changing your hair from straight to wavy or curly.

Hair Alternatives—Wigs, Weaves and Extensions

There are times in a woman's life when she would like a new 'do without sacrificing her own hair. This is where hair alternatives—wigs, hairpieces and hair weaves—are very useful.

Hair alternatives are an answer to a woman's hair prayer. With hair alternatives you can keep your own hair color or length while you experiment with different looks, styles and colors. Women who have wigs, hairpieces or hair weaves in their personal hairstyle collection are in hair heaven. These women have found a way to create different looks while maintaining their own hair.

To care for your wigs, weaves or extensions, Frieda recommends you first find out what they are made of. Some are made with natural hair and others with synthetics. Once you find out how they are made, you should follow the manufacturer's instructions for caring for your hair alternatives.

What to Do About Hair Loss?

If your hair is supposed to be your crowning glory, then what do you do when you are losing it or have lost it? This is a very sensitive topic for many women. When a woman loses her hair, it can result in emotional damage or low self-esteem because she may feel unattractive.

Hair loss or female baldness can be a result of many things, including heredity, thinning hair as we age, medications or chemotherapy. Regardless of the reason, if you are a woman experiencing hair loss, consult with your hairstylist on various ways to adapt your hairstyle with either wigs or hair extensions.

Frieda recommends you first see a dermatologist to find the root of the problem. A dermatologist can analyze your scalp to discover the causes of your hair loss.

Once you discover the problem, work with your dermatologist and hairstylist so that, together, they can find the best hair care treatment and the hairstyle that is right for you.

For those women who have chosen to flaunt their baldness, we applaud you for your stance and boldness—you are truly unique and attractive, creating your style your way.

Choosing the Right Hairstylist

With the hundreds of hairstylists out there, how do you choose the one who is right for you? Consider the following in making your decision:

- Years of experience
- Referrals
- Professionalism
- Personality
- Good listener

Ready for a New 'Do? Get Ready for a New You!

As you reflect on the choices you have to achieve a new hairstyle and boost your confidence, consider the following questions and fill in the blanks:

1. I want my hair to be _____.
2. I want to have a _____ look.
3. If my hairstyle were the answer to my feelings, then I would want to feel _____.
4. I want my colleagues/clients to see me as _____.
5. I want a hairstyle that is _____.
6. If my hair had a voice, I would like it to say_____.

As you write the answers to these questions, you will unlock the courage to change, update or transform your hairstyle and create a new you, your style, your way—your hair of distinction.

RONDA ANDERSON, MA, AICI FLC
Distinguished Impressions

Creating visible credibility

(678) 999-8031
ronda@distinguishedimpressions.com
www.distinguishedimpressions.com

Ronda Anderson is founder of Distinguished Impressions, an image consulting company that specializes in professional grooming standards for men and women. She teaches others how to package and present themselves to make a "mark of distinction" in their workplace, ministry and social environment.

With 30 years of experience in the fashion retail industry, Ronda teaches visual presentation skills to increase the confidence, credibility and self-esteem of others.

The mission of Distinguished Impressions is to assist leaders in achieving inner and outer beauty using grooming essentials for the spirit, soul and body while maintaining an appearance that is positive, professional and fashionable. In this way, they can achieve favorable results and make a lasting impression.

Ronda enjoys having the opportunity to improve and enhance the appearance of others. Her individual consultations and image workshops will show you the keys to making your "image price tag" consistent with your expertise, career objectives, business and social status.

The Unseen Essentials of Style

By Connie Elder

**"To put it bluntly, I seem to have a whole superstructure
with no foundation. But I'm working on the foundation."**
—Marilyn Monroe, American actress, singer and model

A few years ago, I was preparing to celebrate my fortieth birthday in style. As I was getting ready to put on my new LBD (little black dress), I realized I owned a fabulous "superstructure wardrobe" but I was definitely lacking in the "foundation wardrobe." I rushed out to shop for something to hide the lumps and bumps I hadn't noticed when I bought the dress. To my amazement, the selection in the lingerie department only made me look worse in the dress.

The year was 1998, and the choices for shaping undergarments were extremely limited. "Girdle" was a term still in use at that time, and described a form of torture as much as it referred to undergarment support. Bras offered in larger cup sizes were far from attractive, and the selection was sparse. Strapless bras that actually worked for a larger bust were virtually non-existent, except in the form of a "long-line" bra. When I realized how stark the choices were, I decided to create a line of functional and fashionable foundation choices in order to give women better options. Through years of experience giving women a strong foundation to looking great, I have learned quite a lot, and in the following pages I will demystify the topic of your invisible essential style ingredient and share with you the tools to enable you to always look your best.

First Things First: You Are Not Alone!

You are probably like most women—you have a closet full of fabulous clothes. And like many women, do you not wear most of your wardrobe because you don't like the way you look in your clothes? As we age, our bodies change, and the changes are different for each of us. Some women gain weight after childbirth, during menopause, after they get married . . . the list goes on. Some women lose weight as they age, after a divorce, for health reasons or by choice. These bodily changes alter the way your clothes fit, which can wreak havoc on your appearance and your wardrobe choices, not to mention your clothing budget. This is why you need to reevaluate your foundation wardrobe—or build one if you haven't already. It is an essential part of developing your best personal style.

Your first layer of style is your foundation, or what you place next to your skin—your shapewear and bra. Whether you shop at Nordstrom® or Target®, or your style is formal, business or casual, you can develop a more flattering image with smart undergarments that accentuate your body type and bring out your true style.

When the seasons change, most women find themselves sequestered in their closet, having a private fashion show. They try on each of their favorite pieces from the past season to see if it can stay or be updated with accessories, or if it needs to move on to a donation pile. The area of the closet or the drawer that is overlooked most often during this process is the place you keep your shapewear, bras and undies. This is a prime time to update, streamline and purge your underwear drawer. Make a date with yourself at least once a year to eliminate the bad, old, worn out, doesn't fit, when-I-lose-10-pounds, wouldn't-want-to-be-seen-in undies! You will be amazed at how you can decrease the time it takes to get dressed each day. You will find the right pieces for each outfit because you will only have "good" ones.

Have you lost weight, or have you gained weight? Are there pieces you have not worn in years? Can you see visible signs of wear and tear on some pieces? Does it still hold you up or hold you in? These are essential questions to help you decide if the piece can stay or go.

That favorite bra of yours, the one you probably wear more than the others, is almost always the one that needs replacing! The number of bras, shapewear and underwear you are rotating will determine the life span of each piece. An average life span for underwear of any kind is about six to twelve months at the most, based on normal use. If you have a strapless bra you wear twice a year, this rule does not apply. It may need replacing due to weight gain or loss, but not as a result of wear and tear. Getting dressed is easier if each piece of underwear in your wardrobe fits—today. Make room for foundation garments that reinforce confidence in the woman you see in the mirror. Maximize your current wardrobe by simply having good, effective undergarments.

Intimate Apparel Shopping—My Way

The lingerie department in a large department store can be intimidating. No one over forty enjoys having someone in their twenties assist them with intimate apparel. After all, can she really know how gravity affects a mature woman? A boutique that specializes in intimate apparel will usually have more qualified consultants to assist you with a proper fit. They will often take more time and be more understanding of your concerns.

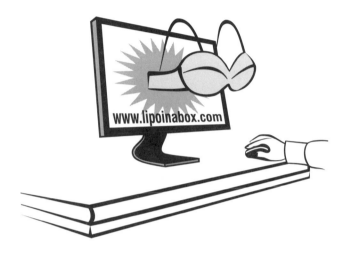

Today, women are finding that shopping online or on television shopping channels like QVC or HSN can be a great way to become informed about and purchase intimate apparel. Reading other opinions on what works for their particular body type is especially helpful in product and brand selection. This can be done from the privacy of your home—after all, it is called "intimate apparel" for a reason. There are websites, blogs and message boards that discuss the many brands of shapewear, bras and other intimate apparel products. Customer reviews will usually give you a non-biased opinion regarding the items you are considering. Some of these websites have customer service available, not just an answering service, with real women who know about the specific products and can provide answers to your individual questions. It's a wonderful way to educate yourself without the possibility of embarrassment.

When I was considering developing and marketing women's undergarments, great customer service was my goal. Every woman views herself as having figure flaws. When looking for solutions to these perceived figure flaws, all of us want—and deserve—to have someone take us seriously and offer valuable advice. You will feel better about undergarment purchases if you can work with caring and knowledgeable staff.

My Shapewear—My Way

When I first developed Lipo in a Box® Shapewear, the tagline was, "This is NOT your Grandma's Girdle." We wanted women to understand that if they owned anything that resembles a girdle, help was on the way.

There have been great strides in intimate apparel in the past ten years: Grandma's girdle has evolved into sleek, comfortable shapewear. There is absolutely no reason to be uncomfortable in your foundation garments. When developing Lipo in a Box shapewear, our strict criteria included comfort, control and confidence. Consider these three factors when making your undergarment selections.

The new shapewear revolution provides solutions to many fashion and figure dilemmas. There are occasions when you select a shapewear style to accent the outfit, while on other occasions it is your body type or the season of the year that dictates your choice.

In the past, many women wore bodysuits as a foundation garment. The trend moved away from bodysuits because the girdle-style bodysuit did not stretch lengthwise. For most women, it either bunched at the waist if you were shorter or wasn't long enough to wear comfortably if you were taller. Be aware that some bodysuits are still made this way. When you are shopping for a bodysuit, make sure it stretches in all directions. When you find one that does, you will love living in your new, second skin! A seamless garment is the best choice when buying a bodysuit, and a seamless bodysuit is undetectable under all your fashion choices. It can be your best kept secret for looking younger and more toned in your clothes.

Lipo in a Box was one of the first brands to make a high-waisted shaper. Today, you will find many brands of high-waist products. This style is very popular if you want to wear your own bra or a strapless bra, if you feel too confined in a full bodysuit, or if you want to spend less money. When selecting a high-waist shaper, be sure it comes all the way up and tucks underneath your bra. This will prevent it from rolling and leaving a gap between your bra and your shaper. Again, selecting a seamless garment is best if you want to be undetectable, especially with light-colored or fine-gauge fabrics.

Bodysuits or high-waist shapers will provide you with a firmer looking midriff area and also eliminate "back fat." Further, if you combine these with a great fitting bra, you will look pounds thinner and years younger in minutes.

If you don't already have a shapewear wardrobe, now is the time to start building one. Shapewear makes it easy to dress with confidence every day. Never again will you need to worry about how you look, whether coming or going. Clothes will drape better on your body. You can be nipped and tucked with no recovery time or scars.

My Bras—My Way

Very few women wear the same size bra at 40 as they did at 30. Wearing the correct size bra is very important. When you wear the correct size bra, there is greater distance between your bust line and your belly button. Women often describe themselves as short-waisted, and in most cases this can be corrected by simply raising the bust line with a proper fitting bra. Other benefits include immediately appearing taller, thinner and younger.

Are you in denial about your cup size? As women age, it can be beneficial to wear a larger cup size, which will contain the breast tissue better and prevent the "double bubble" look in your clothes. A smooth, full-coverage bra is a must-have staple for your foundation wardrobe. Many bras today are designed to provide full coverage with a nice plunging neckline. Both features are very important to complement current fashion trends.

In the past, there was a limited selection of bras for larger cup sizes. Due in part to baby boomers aging and widespread breast augmentation, we are experiencing improvement in this area. A few years after launching Lipo in a Box shapewear, my customers asked me to consider developing a bra line for larger-busted women. Being a larger-busted woman myself, I certainly understood the need and lack of choices in bras for larger cup sizes. Go2 Bras® was created for this purpose and specializes in C to DDD cup sizes, with a few B cups and G cups.

When it comes to bra sizing, you must remain flexible. Try to step out of your comfort zone with the size you think you are and try a few different sizes. Bra sizing is not consistent, even within the same brand. The style of the bra can make it fit differently depending on your body shape and bust type. You may have different band and cup sizes in your bra wardrobe at any given time.

Be more concerned with the fit of the bra than with the size on the label. You want the cups to contain your entire bust—top, bottom and sides—without any puckering. If you have one breast that is larger than the other, fit the larger breast. There are products that can be used to fill in the smaller cup and provide modesty too. Make sure the band size is tight enough to raise your bust line up and off your ribcage. Look for non-stretch straps, because this will provide more support for a larger bust and make the bra last longer. The back of your bra should not be riding up; it should stay in place once it is hooked. This will give the appearance of a longer, leaner torso. Nothing will age you more than low-hanging breasts.

Modesty and Shaping Products—My Way

SMART CUPS™ are bra inserts designed for modesty and shaping. They can be used inside a thinner bra for modesty without adding bulk. The inserts are an excellent choice for bras without padding, shelf camis, sports bras and swimwear. Most women have a smaller breast on one side, and these products are very useful when you would like to fill in the smaller side. Another frequent use for inserts is to fill in a bra when one has undergone a lumpectomy, causing one side of your bra to not fit as snugly.

Foundation Care—My Way

Once you build your foundation wardrobe, you must care for it differently than other clothing. It is best to hand-wash your foundation garments. If this does not work for your lifestyle, you may place your undergarments in a mesh laundry bag and use your washing machine's gentle cycle. Never dry your foundation garment in the dryer! Most foundation garments contain spandex, and dryer heat will break down the spandex and shorten the life of your garments.

Tip: Forever New® is a great detergent for intimate apparel.

Skin Care—My Way

Just as your shapewear provides the perfect foundation for all your fabulous fashions, good skin is what provides the perfect canvas for your makeup. Without good skin, you can easily end up using too much makeup, with unnatural-looking results. Be sure to read Brenda Azevedo's chapter, *Wake Up Your Makeup*, on page 121, for great tips on what to put on top of your great skin.

The most important thing to look for in skin care is a short ingredients list. If a product has fabulous active ingredients and the ingredients are diluted with many inactive ingredients, how much benefit are you really going to experience? Many companies use the latest and greatest active ingredients, which are expensive, and then dilute them with inexpensive fillers. This allows them to use the active ingredients in marketing materials, but at the expense of their customers' satisfaction. Consumers are often misled by this type of advertising; it is important to read the labels and understand the ingredients in products you apply to your skin. If a company touts an active ingredient for a product, yet the ingredient does not appear at the top of the list, you are unlikely to experience the benefits of that ingredient.

The quickest way to improve your skin is to give it attention. If you have great skin care products under your bathroom sink and are not using them, they cannot help your skin! This may sound elementary, but skin care products must be used routinely to be effective.

To-Do List:

a.m.
wash face
_____
_____
_____
_____

p.m.
wash face
_____
_____
_____
_____
_____

Skin care regimens do not have to be complicated. Daily use of a gentle cleanser, an anti-aging peptide or hydrating serum, day and night moisturizers (along with a product specifically for the sensitive area around the eyes), will keep your skin looking better than most. The key is using it consistently. There are many wonderful specialty products available that can enhance the appearance of your skin and slow down the aging process, if you choose to invest the time and money.

Sunscreen, sunscreen, sunscreen . . . did I mention sunscreen? Use it. The damage from the sun on your skin is cumulative. Statistics say one in five people will get skin cancer. Use sunscreen when driving, in the winter and even when you don't think you need it. Sun damage is the primary cause of wrinkles and premature aging. When you attend your class reunions, you will be glad you used lots of sunscreen.

Most of us think of our faces when we think of skin care. Keep in min.. your skin is the largest organ of your body. Make sure you take care of all of your skin! Hydration is the key to younger-looking skin.

Tip: www.underology.com—pure, clean skin care, short ingredients list, high-tech active ingredients and reasonably priced. Also may be found at www.QVC.com.

Style and beauty are built on a *firm foundation.* Take what we have discussed here and shore up yours to always look your best.

CONNIE ELDER
Connie Elder International

*We make you look good
with your clothes on*

**(615) 885-1800
info@lipoinabox.com
www.lipoinabox.com**

Connie Elder is one of the key innovators in the modern shapewear industry. While she was preparing to celebrate her 40th birthday, she realized she didn't have a solution to help her fit into the fabulous dress she bought for the occasion—and she discovered a prime opportunity for women like her.

Since then, Connie has developed hundreds of popular products through several product lines: Underology Skin Care,™ Go2 Bras™ and Lipo in a Box,™ which have been featured on *The Oprah Winfrey Show, The View, Today, The Early Morning Show* at CBS and in many magazines and best-selling fashion books.

Connie has also been the on-air spokesperson on QVC Shopping Channel for Lipo in a Box since 2002, and in the Spring of 2010, Connie introduced Go2 Bras and Underology Skin Care to the popular home shopping community.

Connie is very active in supporting charitable causes, including Breast Cancer Research and Shelters for Victims of Domestic Violence. Connie also serves on the board of directors for Soles4Souls, Inc. and the YWCA Nashville. You can learn more about Connie, her products and the causes close to her heart by visiting www.lipoinabox.com.

The Diva Is in the Details

Personal Details and Finishing Touches

By Teca Cameron

Have you ever seen a woman walk into a room and been automatically captivated by her presence? I mean, she just drew attention and radiated without seeming to exert even the slightest bit of effort? You find yourself trying to figure it out—is it the way she walks? Perhaps it's her manner of speech. Maybe it's the colors that she wears? Is it the way she lifts her head ever so slightly to let others know that she is listening attentively to their cares? What is it that makes her so captivating?

If you haven't seen such a woman, I can assure you that I have. This is a woman who takes care of the "small stuff" because she knows that those minor details are what makes the difference between "ho-hum" and "so glam." I have noticed that there are many women who possess this natural radiance. While they possess signature style and presence, sometimes they just need a little bit of tweaking to make it work to their advantage and make their Diva shine.

What do I mean by "Diva"? Many people associate "Diva-ism" with eccentric, self-absorbed and sometimes self-righteous be-havior. I associate being a Diva with knowing who you are as a woman and making no excuses for being ever so fabulous.

A Diva in my eyes is a woman who is confident, self-assured, and a smart risk-taker who knows what she wants out of life. When it comes to her style, it is all her own. Like an artist in front of a canvas, she dibbles and dabbles with style formulas until she gets it just right—just right for her, that is.

In this chapter, I am going to teach you about the finer details of style. You can radiate naturally by taking care of the small things. Simply put, knowing how to personalize your style and paying attention to details is really what will give you that memorable and distinguishing radiance that is often reserved for the greatest of celebrities—and we all know that celebrities have nothing on you! When you are walking out the door, leave no detail untouched. The world ought to recognize the power of your presence.

Your Diva Mane

How does a Diva ensure that her hair is always current? The first step is getting to understand your hair. We might look at other people and desire to have hairstyles that they have, but by doing so, we tend to forget or not realize that our hair, lifestyle and face shape is not the same as theirs. What works for her may not be the best style for you.

When looking for a new hairstyle, ask yourself the following questions:

- What is my hair texture (straight, curly, wavy; fine or thick; dry, oily or normal)?
- What is my face shape (round, diamond, square, oblong, oval, heart)?
- What kind of hairstyle can I live with for my lifestyle and budget (short, long, chemically altered, natural)?

Once you figure these things out, find out how you can wear your hair naturally to keep it in its best shape. I encourage taking risks with hairstyles because there are so many options if you are willing to experiment.

If you are going to take risks with your hair, choose a style that is flattering to the shape of your face, make sure it is suitable for your lifestyle (high or low maintenance) and make sure you can live with it if it is drastic.

If you have long hair and want to try a new style, try using a hairstyling software program, get a hair consultation or purchase a short wig. Another option would be to have your hairstylist "weave" your hair and then cut the extensions into a short style. This minimizes the risk that you will have a hairstyle you simply cannot live with and gives you an easy out if you want to go back to wearing your hair the way it was.

African-American hair. I wish to highlight African-American hair because we have unique challenges and blessings when it comes to our hair texture.

First of all, if your vocabulary includes any of the following words, I am pleading with you to eliminate them from your mind and your mouth: nappy, rough, bad, awful, disgusting, poor quality and picky. You would be surprised how much our hair will choose to work against us when we curse it.

I say this with the greatest amount of respect and adoration. I grew up disliking my hair and used to think surely there was a major crisis at the hair factory on the day God chose to produce my hair, because under no circumstances would God have been so cruel. I mean, any word that was negative would be hurled out of my mouth at my hair. Guess what: in return, my hair did not appreciate me. We had fights, I threw tantrums, I put my hair and myself through hell trying to make it do things that it could not do because those things were simply against its nature.

When I learned to appreciate and care for my hair for what it was—which I now know is beautiful, thick, versatile and luscious—I was amazed at how much it flourished.

Whether you want to wear a natural afro, twist your hair into locks or chemically alter it, do what you think is best. I really encourage women to wear their hair as natural as possible or to choose extensions to cover their hair rather than use chemicals. With the prevalence of diseases such as cancer and the stress that comes with chemically altering our hair, I just can't see anything good coming from the process. Nonetheless, to each her own.

Your hair is your beauty. Adorn your tresses with a touch of flair, keep your hair healthy and stay current with your look. If you color your hair, pay attention to getting your roots touched up, and be sure to choose a color that is right for your complexion. A color analysis really helps with narrowing down your hair color options.

Your Diva Regimen

Much like hair care, I encourage you to take good care of your skin, teeth and body. Skin care regimens really depend on your individual skin type and your lifestyle. As a fan of all things natural, I encourage using natural products to care for your face and body. I know that products with chemicals are more readily available, but it can actually work out to be cheaper and healthier to go the natural route. We probably can't eliminate the use of chemicals, although we can make efforts to minimize the number of chemicals to which we expose ourselves. As someone with combination skin, my favorite skin care products include avocado, honey, apricot and mint scrubs, clay masks, oatmeal, water vapors, vitamin C and aloe vera. Consider getting a blender and experimenting with different ingredients. Learn about the health properties of each ingredient and how the nutrients it contains can help you meet your skin care and beauty needs.

A basic skin care regimen includes twice-daily facial washing, exfoliating (using a gentle skin scrub), toner and moisturizer. I love to indulge in a good fruit acid facial every now and then. The feeling of being pampered is like none other—especially after an exhausting day. If you can afford it, I recommend regular visits to an esthetician who will exfoliate and mask your skin. If you can do this for yourself, then I strongly encourage you to make this a regular part of your skin care regimen.

Eye cream made from rich nutrients such as vitamin C and vitamin K are essential. Raccoon eyes, under-eye bags and crow's feet are all unflattering. Your eyes are the windows to your soul; treat the surrounding area with love and care.

Your Diva Scent

Pay very close attention to your hygiene and, if you tend to occupy enclosed spaces regularly throughout the day and are in the company of others, use fewer scented products. Experiment with fruit and natural scents. I love to use scents such as peach, chocolate, vanilla or any other yummy flavor. Do explore—and keep your scent soft, feminine and flirty.

Your Diva Smile

A Diva's smile is her passport to possibilities. If you have a great smile, you will have better interpersonal relations. People gravitate to a pleasing demeanor. Keep your smile pearly white and in great shape. A daily regimen of flossing, brushing and cleansing your mouth will keep you on track for well-groomed teeth. If you have dental issues, consider a trip to your dental surgeon and ask him or her for recommendations on how to get the most out of your smile. Dental work can be expensive, especially if it is cosmetic. However, I can assure you that a minor change in your smile can have a major impact on your appearance and will provide a great return on your investment.

If your teeth are discolored, consider using baking soda as a natural substitute for toothpaste to whiten your teeth. Also, avoid excessive amounts of caffeinated drinks, red wine and foods that tend to lead to dental discoloration. If you must go the chemical route, there are many products on the market that can whiten teeth. Ask your dentist which ones will work best for your teeth.

Your Diva Vessel

To look your very best on the outside, it is so important to take good care of yourself on the inside. Before anything else, take your eating habits into consideration. Eat as healthily as you possibly can within your personal budget. It is difficult to do with our busy lifestyles these days, but it is so important. Many of the ailments that plague our society stem from our neglect of our bodies. Find an eating plan that works for your lifestyle, contains healthy food choices and is relatively easy to prepare.

Consider cooking fresh foods, eating plenty of fruits and veggies and drinking plenty of water. Your skin will glow, your hair and nails will be in great shape and best of all, you will feel great.

I also encourage you to take up a sport, walk, sign up for the gym, swim, garden—do some physical activity to keep your body in check. I am not a huge fan of the gym, so I try to find other ways to give myself a cardiovascular workout. Whatever you choose to do, just keep your body in tip-top shape. When you are fit, you feel fabulous. When you feel fabulous, you look fabulous. When you look fabulous, you live a fabulous life. Diva, it's all about being fabulous!

Undergarments. Although you try to keep your body fit, sometimes you need a little bit of help. Well, the first thing I recommend is finding out your correct bra size and wearing a bra that provides appropriate support. Without one, you risk having your precious gems fall toward the floor sooner than you would probably desire. A well-lifted bustline is very flattering in any outfit. It gives you the appearance of excellent posture—another distinguishing feature of a Diva.

Since we are on the topic of undergarments, let's talk about VPLD—Visible Panty Line Disorder. By my observation, this disorder affects one in five women. I encourage you to leave those panty lines in the panty drawer. Seamless underwear or thong panties are the key to eliminating the visible panty line. Imagine you are dressed to the nines, but one small—yet relatively critical—aspect of your attire is overlooked and you are walking with one half of your underwear hitched in places it shouldn't be and the other half visibly covering the other cheek. Everyone but you can see the secrets that Victoria tried to keep for you. A mistake like this will take your look from hot to not-so-hot in a split second.

Also, don't be afraid of body shapers. They can really hold in some parts that we would rather not put on display. There are so many options on the market; be daring and give one a shot. For more about shapewear, see Connie Elder's chapter, *The Unseen Essentials of Style,* on page 147.

Dressing for your shape. This area of detail is so critical that we've devoted an entire chapter to the subject: see *Be True to Your Shape,* by Johonna Duckworth, on page 61. There is no greater way to show attention to detail than demonstrating that you understand your own unique design. Find out what your body type is. Learn what types of clothes you should wear for your body's type and weight and what types of fabrics work best for your build. Make these your staples.

It is a simple manner of dressing, and it won't cost you a lot of money. As a matter of fact, it will actually save you quite a lot, and you will be able to appreciate your figure even more because you accept it for what it is.

This acceptance ultimately leads to self-confidence, which you will discover is the secret ingredient behind a Diva's radiance.

Your Diva Flair

I would do this chapter a complete injustice if I did not conclude with a section on how to dress with flair. You've taken care of the details— the significant elements of being and looking well. How do you incorporate all of this into dressing well?

The secret is expanding your imagination and being creative. Get your inspiration from nature, your surroundings, your ancestors, icons, other cultures or even art.

Consider your wardrobe as an artist's toolkit. Your basic clothing items are the bare canvas. When I refer to basic clothing items, I am talking about closet essentials such as pants, jackets, dresses and skirts in the most neutral, classic styles for your figure. These should be of the best quality, and in shades or tones that are flattering to your skin tone.

Build upon this canvas using coloring tools. Be open to wearing vibrant colors that are flattering to your skin tone. Add sweaters, blouses or tops that are rich in patterns, textures, colors or details. Don't be afraid of florals, polka dots, ruffles, lace, embroidery, abstract patterns, checks, studs or chains. The possibilities are endless.

The art of dressing well is understanding that your ability to coordinate outfits containing contrasting details is really what separates you from the pack. Anyone can throw on a solid blouse and a plain pencil skirt. As a Diva, you could instead opt for a blouse in rich colors and perhaps a vibrant print, your handbag might be a quality statement satchel, your jewels bold yet chic, and your shoes would accent your outfit by playing up one of the colors from your blouse.

To add the finishing touches, go crazy with your accessories—jewelry, handbags and shoes. Don't be afraid to be bold.

Wear jewelry that is pleasing to your size, personal taste and body frame. Consider wearing statement jewelry, as these pieces can take an outfit from dull to Diva in a nanosecond. I suggest experimenting with trendy jewelry because that keeps you current.

Handbags are an essential tie-in piece. Polish off a look with a handbag appropriate for the occasion. There is no requirement to carry a Birkin® bag to be a Diva, but surely if it is Birkin-like, it should be in good shape, look expensive and, most important, represent you.

Let us not forget the shoes. You have probably heard the saying that a woman can never have too many shoes. No truer statement has been made. An argument can almost always be made to justify why a particular shoe is an essential requirement in a woman's wardrobe—especially a Diva's.

When selecting shoes, consider the following: where you are going, what is more important—comfort or style, will they last and does the price equal value for money? If you choose comfort, I suggest you keep your choice modern and as "unfrumpy" as possible. With the options that are available, from flats to wedges, from kitten heels to sky-high stilettos, there are myriad possibilities.

A few of my own rules for shoes:

- **If it does not fit—we must leave it!** Simply put, your toes should not be crawling over your shoes to hit the floor, and your heel should fit comfortably on the back of your shoe. Shoes that are too tight can cause many foot issues, including calluses, corns and the dreaded B word—bunions. A poor fit can also affect your posture and blood circulation. End of story—find shoes that fit.

- **Splurging on trendy shoes is less than a bright idea.** Unless you can afford to buy a new shoe the moment it hits the shelves or the Internet, keep trendy picks thrifty.

- **Give attention to your feet if they will be showing.** If you wear sandals or sling-back, open-toe or peep-toe shoes, please ensure that your feet are well taken care of. Your toenails and heels require attention. Consider getting or giving yourself regular pedicures. If time is a factor, cuticle oil, lotion, nail clippers and a nail file should suffice. It is really against the Diva Code to walk on heels that are thick and as coarse as bricks. Please moisturize; your shoes and your audience will love you for it.

To finish off any look, it is important to remember: the Diva walks with her head straight, captivates with a signature sway in her hip, invites with a smile and radiates confidence, flair and class.

Claim Your Diva

Paying attention to detail is such an important part of looking and feeling fantastic. Your hair, scent, beauty regimen, smile, body care and signature style are all so important in the art of being well put together.

Life is too short to settle for mediocrity. Try taking bold risks with style, venture outside of your comfort zone and most importantly, keep an eye out for the details.

There is a Diva in you. Go ahead—work your magic and stay fabulous!

TECA CAMERON
Teca Cameron Image Management Agency

Reflect. Transform. Radiate

(416) 342-9577
info@tecacameron.com
www.tecacameron.com
www.stelladot.com/tecacameron

Teca is an image consultant based in Canada. She specializes in working with individuals and organizations to identify their unique branding formula.

Teca offers services in color analysis, personal shopping, style coaching/assessment, and wardrobe audit and analysis. She also conducts workshops and seminars on business communication, leadership and workplace etiquette. As a Self Image coach, Teca works with her clients to develop positive self-perceptions and confidence.

You can say it's in her DNA. Teca grew up with family members who had confidence and a strong sense of style, and were fashionable in their own unique ways. They all had one thing in common—they were her inspiration for fashion, style and all things related to beauty. From adolescence, Teca loved to give fashion advice to all who would listen. Fashion and beauty are her first loves.

Teca obtained an honours bachelor of administrative studies degree from York University and an Image Consulting Certificate from George Brown College, where she studied with Karen Brunger. Teca is an active member of the Association of Image Consultants International.

Dressing for Dating Success
The Secret of Attracting the Man You Want

By Sheila Dicks, CEG

"Know, first, who you are; and then adorn yourself accordingly."
—Epictetus, Greek philosopher

Most women care very much about how they look, and when it comes to dating, they know that men are visual creatures and image is important. However, they are not clear about the connection between attraction and image. They spend loads of money on clothes and cosmetics but they do it haphazardly. Very few women put much time into learning how to look their best. They get caught up in the latest trends and, for the most part, believe that owning a designer dress, bag or jacket will in some way make them more appealing. They don't put any time into learning which styles, colors and designs accentuate their features and look best on them. No one has ever found her signature style by following magazines, observing celebrities or emulating someone else.

So how does this play out when it comes to dating? Many women go all out when they are in search of their Prince Charming; others don't give a hoot. Those who dress to attract a man usually send their Prince Charming in the other direction or they attract the wrong type. This usually happens because they are not dressing from who they are but rather who they believe they should be.

The woman who says she doesn't care how she looks or dresses, and says that her Mr. Right won't care how she looks, runs into a major problem. Her "ideal man," the person who has all that she is looking for, is usually "Mr. Perfect," a man who is suave and impeccably dressed. The problem is that he will not be attracted to a woman who doesn't care enough to be well-groomed. He will walk right on by and she will be left with "Mr. Good Enough" or nobody.

As a result, many women will tell you that Mr. Right is not out there. Why? Because they have been going about finding him in all the wrong ways. They haven't learned the power of image and the message that developing your personal image sends.

What effect does your image have on the men you attract? How can you develop a signature style that is all yours and brings in the man you want? We will address those questions and more in this chapter. No matter what your age or how you dress now, it is never too late to tweak your image and attract Mr. Right into your life.

The Most Important First Step

Before we go any further, it's time to stop and evaluate where and who you are in the dating arena. While it is true that how you dress has a huge impact on the type of man you attract, we cannot forget this one important fact: you will attract a person who is in harmony with who you really are— not the person you say you are. Make a list of all the character traits you would like in a man, and then ask yourself—and answer honestly or it won't work—how many of those traits you possess. For example, many women make the mistake of looking for a man who will be good to them and treat them well, while they are very unkind to themselves. They frequently put themselves down (I'm not good enough, not smart enough, too fat, too whatever) and/or disrespect themselves by putting up with bad behavior from others.

If you are a person who continually attracts men who are abusive, you might want to spend some time uncovering your unconscious beliefs before you proceed any further. However, if you know that your style is holding you back, then it's time for a change.

Messages Clothes Send

Clothing is viewed by people in many ways. It can be seen as a way to keep warm or cool; it can make certain activities easier, as when wearing the right shoes or pants; it can be a way to show off how much money you have; it can attract the opposite sex or it can be a way to blend in and not be noticed. There are as many functions as there are people.

When clothes are worn to attract the opposite sex, we have to become aware of the messages our clothes send and whether it is the message we want to send. I find that even women who have a good grasp on how to dress—that is, how to match colors and styles—sometimes continue to choose clothes that send the wrong message. Let's explore some of the messages clothes send.

- **Available.** Let's get this one out of the way at the onset. If you dress as though you are available—you wear plunging necklines or short skirts or bare a lot of skin—you will be sure to get lots of dates. Yes, lots and lots of dates, but no more than that. Here's the contradiction:

even though men love and are attracted to women who ooze sex appeal, they don't want to keep them. Okay, let me back up. Men do like sexiness but they want it only for themselves. Meaning, after you have made the connection and are in a monogamous relationship, bring it on! However, while you're still dating—Mr. Right, that is—if you have listed one of Mr. Right's attributes as respectful, he won't be interested if you flaunt your sexiness and appear available for everyone.

- **Standoffish.** This trait does not only show itself in dress, but also in demeanor. A person who is standoffish wears professional clothes in a leisure environment. For example, a woman who goes out on a first date dressed in a suit or something equally professional is sending the message that she is all business and that she views dating as a business deal. She appears to have a cool exterior and, instead of Mr. Right being attracted to her, he is scared away by her chilly, businesslike exterior. Most men are looking for warmth from a woman, someone who can drop business and quickly move into a womanly role. A respectable man is interested in women who see him as an equal and a companion.

- **Uninterested.** It's surprising how many women dress this way when they are anything but uninterested. The woman who appears uninterested is a sloppy dresser. She goes on a date without makeup, with untidy hair, wearing baggy jeans or an old T-shirt. Her motto is, "This is who I am and I'm not going to dress up for anyone." As I said before, with this thinking, please don't expect to meet Mr. Right, if you see your Mr. Right as well-groomed, polished and successful.

- **Approachable.** Finally, we've come to the message you will want to send. A woman who appears approachable dresses in a way that suits her personality and the occasion. She pays close attention to details and is always well groomed. Let's take a look at the essentials of an approachable look.

The Essentials: Cut and Color

Dressing for successful dating is much like dressing for success in any area of life in that it involves paying careful attention to details. Whether you love to wear dresses or pants, to obtain the look you desire, carefully consider the cut and color of each clothing piece and how it adorns your body.

Cut. The cut of clothing refers to the shape or silhouette of a garment. The cut and fabric of a garment will determine how it hangs and how it looks. For example, pants can have straight legs, wide legs, narrow legs, pleats and a high or low waist. Getting to know your body shape will help you select the most flattering style. Unless you have a perfectly proportioned body, not all of these pant styles will look great. However, no matter what your shape, at least one style will look better than others. It is essential to determine which cut will look best on you. For more on dressing for your shape, see Johonna Duckworth's chapter, *Be True to Your Shape,* on page 61.

Why should this matter? Choosing clothing pieces that bring out your best features will create a favorable appearance.

Color. So much has been written about the power of color that I am surprised more people don't use it to their advantage. Of all the aspects of creating a stunning image, color and how you use it has the greatest effect on how you look. When you discover which colors look best on you and wear them consistently, you will notice that you feel and look much better.

We instinctively know and are drawn to colors that look best on us though we are sometimes swayed, against our better judgment, by fashion trends and the opinions of others. That is why it is important to use our natural instincts and take into consideration our hair, eye and skin colors to find the best colors for us to wear.

It is ideal to seek out the services of a color professional to find your best colors. However, the first step in finding your best colors is to discover whether you are in the warm or cool category. Cool colors are blue-based and look best if your hair color is black, dark brown, grey or white, light brown or silver grey; your eye color is brown, green, hazel, or soft blue.

Examples of cool colors include blue-based red, emerald green, royal blue, burgundy and purple.

Warm colors are yellow-based and look best if your hair color is strawberry blonde, ash blonde, auburn, dark red, copper or honey blonde; your eye color is brown, green, olive, teal blue or blue-grey.

Examples of warm colors are olive, teal blue, coral, orange, camel and cream.

Color also has a psychological effect; it affects how you feel and is the first thing others see when they look at you. This is why it is important to choose colors that look great on you, and to use them to create the effect you'd like.

Red stirs up emotions and is associated with passion, energy, desire and love; pink (the light side of red) signifies romance, love and friendship. Green is the color of nature and is associated with growth, fertility and harmony. Orange produces a feeling of energy and is a color that people love or hate. Red-orange produces a need for action and pleasure. Blue is associated with health, healing and tranquility and has a calming effect. Yellow is often associated with joy, happiness and energy. Purple symbolizes power, luxury and ambition.

Take the power of colors into consideration when you are choosing clothing to dress to attract. For more about choosing colors, see Dawn Stebbing's chapter, *Enhance Your Image with Color,* on page 49.

Radiating Confidence—The Attraction of Being You

What type of presence do you have? Are people naturally drawn to you? Are you seen as an interesting person whom people want to know? Or are you withdrawn and difficult to get to know? Your demeanor and the messages it sends will have a huge impact on how often you are approached. It doesn't matter how impeccably dressed you are, if you are sending out a message of aloofness or a lack of self-confidence, you won't be approached for a date. Let's investigate a few options that you can use to boost your attraction level.

- **Pay attention to nonverbal communication.** Studies show that up to 55 percent of our communication is nonverbal. Our nonverbal communication can be seen in our facial expressions, eye contact, body position, and hand and feet movements.

  In the arena of attraction, the most important nonverbal gesture is a smile. A smile is welcoming and lets people know that you are open to contact.

  Use body language to show confidence. Walk with your head high and your shoulders back. Don't lean, slouch or carry yourself in a hunched position. If you are an introvert, fight the desire to gravitate to the nearest corner; initiate a conversation and introduce yourself to others.

- **Defining your fashion personality.** To determine your unique signature style, begin by discovering your fashion personality. When you dress in concert with your true personality, dressing will be easier and you will feel more at ease and more comfortable. Fashion personalities are broken down into four groups: romantic, sporty, dramatic and classic.

You have a romantic fashion personality if you have a preference for a soft, feminine look and would rather wear dresses and skirts than pants. Your fashion personality is sporty if you feel most comfortable in casual clothes, and love natural woven fabrics and unstructured jackets and cardigans. Your fashion personality is dramatic if you like to wear form-fitting, tailored looks, bold prints and geometric designs. Yours is a classic fashion personality if you like an elegant, traditional look and wear timeless, tailored clothing.

Dressing for the Occasion

Do you dress your best for all occasions, or are you sometimes a little relaxed in how you look? For example, if you are meeting a friend for lunch or going to the theater, you dress well—but if you are scooting out to the supermarket for a loaf of bread or dropping your child off at school, you throw on the first available piece of clothing you pick up off the floor. If you don't always look your best when you are in public, you could be setting yourself up for an embarrassing moment. The fact is, you could meet Mr. Right anywhere. You could meet him while you are getting your tires changed or shopping for furniture, just as easily as when you are ready for him and "dressed to kill."

While standing in front of your closet, give some consideration to the occasion for which you are dressing. Whether you are going to a business meeting, shopping, to church or to a gala event, what you wear should be tailored to fit the occasion. To ensure you always feel at ease and comfortable, choose an outfit that fits well and suits your unique style.

A business setting can be traditional (banking, law, etc.) or softly tailored (advertising, public relations, etc.). The dress code for traditional business is structured, tailored clothes with straight lines and firm fabrics (suits). For a softly tailored business setting, use softer lines, structured blazers and jackets, and matched or unmatched tailored pants.

Social occasions can include anything from lunch with a friend to a formal event. To feel comfortable at an informal social event, opt for unmatched suits, denim skirts, khaki pants and turtlenecks. "Black tie" means formal and "white tie" means ultra formal. For a black tie event, wear a cocktail dress or long gown.

Ready, Set, Go

To get started, select your best styles—those that accentuate your positive features. Enlist the services of an image consultant if you don't know where to begin. Take into consideration your fashion personality and choose styles you most like to wear. You will feel much more comfortable when you select clothing pieces you love rather than those chosen by someone else. Take the time to discover your best colors and spend some time evaluating the message your clothes have been sending and the message you'd like to send . . . to Mr. Right.

SHEILA DICKS, CEG
Fashion Experts Network

Partner · Promote · Prosper

(902) 578-0509
sheila@fashionexpertsnetwork.com
www.fashionexpertsnetwork.com

Sheila is a style and dating coach and the founder of the Fashion Experts Network—an association of image professionals. Sheila is committed to providing men and women the opportunity to create a winning image, gain more self-confidence and reach their personal and business goals.

In 1978, Sheila began her image career as a dressmaker. She has a bachelor of arts in education and has been trained in fashion and beauty. Her curiosity about why people behave the way they do and her keen interest in self-development stimulated many years of study and led her to life coaching. She has helped hundreds of men and women transform their wardrobes, their lives and their self-esteem.

Her quotes and articles have appeared in *Complete Well Being, Home Life, Quilter's Home Magazine, The National Enquirer, Family Journal, The Fresno Bee* and the *Fashion Merchandiser eGuide*. She is co-author of *101 Great Ways to Improve Your Life,* published by Self Improvement Online, Inc. in May 2006.

The Savvy Traveler

By Adena DiTonno

"He who would travel happily must travel light."
—Antoine de St. Exupery, French author

Those of us who are quite confident in our style on a day-to-day basis can become befuddled when it comes to packing for a trip and traveling with effortless style. I used to hate packing for a trip, and I frequently came home from my travels realizing that I had toted along a number of items that I never even wore, or I had forgotten a necessary accessory, rendering some items useless. Needless to say, my husband, who would totally agree with the above "travel light" quote, was always less than thrilled when he saw the big bag I was taking, because he could travel for a couple of weeks with nothing but a carry-on. Now the whole process is much easier for me, because I have a plan of action when I prepare for a trip. That's the goal of this chapter—to answer that all-important question: How can you travel, and prepare to travel, as a savvy traveler with a minimum level of stress?

Savvy Preparation

What is the nature of your trip? Are you traveling to one or maybe two places at most or are you on the move every day or so? Are you meeting girlfriends for a shopping and theater outing, or are you traveling with your husband on a sightseeing excursion? Is there business and pleasure involved? If you are only going to one or two locations or are meeting your girlfriends for a shopping and theater extravaganza, you are probably not going to be as concerned with traveling light and can take more items with you. In fact, in the case of the girlfriends, you may be thinking "more is better!" On the other hand, if you are sightseeing with your husband or are changing locales every few days, you may want to pack more comfortable items and try to put everything you need in one carry-on bag for ease of movement.

Part of the planning process is to consider the climate and planned activities at your destination. A skiing trip will require warmer and possibly heavier clothing, and may require a larger bag. A week on the beach can be enjoyed with lighter-weight items that may easily fit into a carry-on.

Obviously, there can be advantages to one-bag, carry-on packing, such as the security of your belongings, flexibility in the event you need to suddenly change flights, saving time by not waiting in baggage claim to retrieve your bag, and less tipping, because of the reduced need for a porter to help with your belongings, to name a few. Only you can decide if you can manage with one carry-on bag for your travels.

Savvy Planning

Planning what you are going to take with you, and equally impor-tant, what you are *not* going to take with you, is where most of us begin to hyperventilate. If you follow these steps, you can keep your pre-trip stress to a minimum.

- First of all, a few days before you travel, "stage" everything—that is, pull out the items you think you want to take and hang them out in full view, along with accessories, shoes and handbags.

- Organize these items following a daytime and evening schedule— and an afternoon if the activities you have planned will require a clothing change. As you do this, it is important to write down each item. You won't remember all of this later, even though you think you will. You don't have to have a particular form—just use a notepad and write headings like this:

Travel Days	Morning Outfit	Evening Outfit
Monday		
Tuesday		
Wednesday		

- Next, fill it in with the skirts, pants, tops or dresses you'll wear, and their accompanying shoes, handbags, jewelry and any other accessories you may need.

- As you write down the outfits for each day, look for opportunities to repeat or reuse items, without necessarily wearing the same items every day. It usually becomes clear which items are more versatile and useful to you. If something can only be worn once, and you are on a trip that requires carry-on luggage, then put that item aside and look for an item that will serve your purposes and can be worn more than once. Remember that accessories can change the look of the outfit, making it easy to go from casual to dressy. Scarves and jewelry, in particular, work beautifully, and are lightweight and easy to pack.

- Shoes always seem to be an issue for us gals. For carry-on packing, try to pack only two pair of shoes and wear the third. A basic shoe plan would be a pair of black flats, some embellished sandals, and a pair of "dressy" sneakers. If you plan to do a serious workout every day, then forget the dressy sneakers and take your exercise footwear. Because that type of footwear is usually oversized, it will eat up precious room in your carry-on, so that is a consideration. Even if you are checking your bags, as you prepare your daily checklist of outfits, try to utilize each pair of shoes multiple times. Shoes add weight to the bag quickly, which is an important consideration these days when airlines are charging for overweight baggage.

It's so much easier when you travel to refer to the list you've made; you can always change it as you go, and at least you have a plan.

Don't forget:

- **Outerwear if the climate calls for it.** Generally, try to find one basic outerwear garment to accommodate all your activities, if possible. You can carry this onto the plane with you.

- **Any shapewear you may need.** While this may not be an issue for a trip hiking in the mountains, if you are going to be getting dolled up in your favorite satin sheath to go with the girls or your husband to dinner and the theater, you may want that vital piece of shapewear in order to look your best. Sometimes, if there are lots of dress-up opportunities, I take two pieces of shapewear, so that one can be hand washed and hung to dry while I'm wearing the second one.

- **A colorful pashmina**—one of my favorites travel accessories, even when traveling to warm climates—that can be used on the airplane, in chilly restaurants, and, in colder climates, as a neck scarf.

More tips:

- Speaking of handwashing and air-drying, consider taking garments that are synthetic rather than cotton. Synthetics are able to air dry fairly quickly, which can be important when you are changing locales every few days or when you are on a longer trip and need to reuse items. Once you squeeze out the excess water, roll the item in a bath towel and step on it a few times to help further squeeze out moisture. Then unroll the item and hang to dry. You can take packets of Woolite® with you or just use the soap or shower gel in your hotel room to wash out items.

- Consider wearing leggings or knit pants for your travel day. They hold their shape, are comfortable and look very chic.

- Even if your trip is mostly casual, take one special evening piece— you'll be prepared should an interesting invitation emerge.

- Keep in mind airline regulations on allowable size and weight for your carry-on bags, as well as weight limitations for your checked baggage. If your carry-on will require two men to put it into the overhead, you probably overpacked!

- No need to pack your full-blown beauty routine for trips. You can probably survive for a week or so with a shampoo/conditioner combo or you can use the ones in your hotel room. Consider using cleansing wipes, rather than packing full bottles of cleansing lotions. Same goes for day and night moisturizing creams—consider taking only one multi-purpose face cream for use on this short-term basis. This becomes more important when you travel with a carry-on, as all liquid items must fit within that one-quart-sized bag. And even when you are checking baggage, carrying all of your full-sized toiletry items can quickly add weight to your bag, as well as take up a great deal of space. You must decide whether those items are essential or whether you'd rather take an extra pair of shoes!

- Even though it goes without saying, we must say it: do not pack valuables in your checked bag. Specifically, do not pack your money, camera, prescription medicines or jewelry, unless you can afford to lose them. Carry them with you.

Savvy Packing

Various packing methods have their devotees. In general, I recommend one of two ways to pack efficiently: the *alternating garment method*, or the *rolling method*, depending on the type of trip and the type of bag you are taking.

First of all, if you are using a suitcase that provides a side for hanging garments, double-up pants on hangers to save space. Pack every four or so garments in plastic dry-cleaner-type bags to reduce wrinkles.

For the remainder of the suitcase—the deep side—or for a suitcase that has no space for hanging garments, we'll get into the two packing methods mentioned above. I should clarify that there are many variations of these methods, and you can find descriptions and illustrations of them online.

Alternating garment method (sometimes called the bundle method). This is one of the most popular ways to pack wrinkle-free, and works especially well when you are traveling with more dressy or professional wear.

- Line the sides and bottom of the suitcase with shoes, in individual cloth bags ideally, but plastic will do, to protect from scratches.

Shoes can hold socks. Belts can also line the outside edge of the suitcase to take up minimal space.

- First, pack the items that are most likely to wrinkle, such as jackets, dresses and shirts. Lay the first item with its top edge next to one of the long edges of the suitcase and the excess hanging over the remaining three edges of the suitcase. The second item will have its top edge next to the opposite long edge of the suitcase, with its excess also hanging over the remaining three edges. Once all jackets, dresses and shirts have been layered in this alternating fashion, we move on to the other garments.

- Fold your pants and tops lengthwise once. Layer the first item with the waistband of the pant, or neck of the top, next to one of the short edges of the suitcase, with the excess hanging out the other end. The next layer will lay the alternate direction in the bottom, with the ends of that garment hanging outside the opposite end. Continue alternating layers.

- Before you reach the top, lay a plastic bag containing soft items such as underwear and hosiery in the middle of these items.

- Now, begin folding the ends hanging outside of the bag to the inside, garment by garment, until you finish with the bottom items. You'll have a nice bundle that should emerge relatively wrinkle-free.

Rolling method. Another popular method, particularly when you are traveling more casually, is the rolling method. Put shoes on the bottom, around the sides of the suitcase. Fold and lay heavier items, such as jeans or sweaters, on the bottom. Fold all other items once lengthwise and then roll up. Pack them into the suitcase side by side, starting with the bulkier items and moving up to the lightest weight items on top. Pack your suitcase tightly so the items won't loosen up during travel. I used this method recently on a week-long beach vacation and it worked beautifully. You'll find you can take more items this way, or maybe use a smaller suitcase than you normally would.

Savvy Everything Else

- Wear shoes that are easily removable so you won't cause a bottleneck at the TSA screening stations at the airport.

- If you're wearing shoes that don't require socks, consider packing a pair of cotton shoe liners, like Peds®, in the outer pocket of your carry-on. After you've removed your shoes for the screening process, you can slip the Peds on to walk through the screener, and then off again quickly when you put your shoes on—definitely much more sanitary than walking barefoot in the airport screening line.

- Please, as a courtesy to your fellow travelers, be prepared in the security line to pull out your laptop, ideally labeled with your name, and your quart-sized baggie of liquids for separate screening.

- Since we now have access to so much information online, think about downloading information about your destination onto your smart phone or iPad® rather than printing it all out. Likewise, with Internet cafés abounding, load any important documents you need on your trip onto a flash drive and you'll have them at your fingertips.

- We are exposed to many more germs when we travel—just touching the handrail on an escalator, for example. Take packets of Emergen-C® with you and have at least one daily to help fight off "traveler's cold." Likewise, take a small bottle of hand sanitizer and use it frequently.

- In your second carry-on, bring along those magazines that have been stacking up at home—read them and leave them behind as you go. Remember to tear off your name and address; there's no need to leave behind any personal information.

- Scan your important documents—passport, credit cards, and so forth—before you leave. Store them in your web-based email account and email them to yourself. You will be prepared for accessing the info should your documents be lost or stolen.

- It's also a good idea to pack a copy of your itinerary inside your suitcase in case you are separated from your bags; it might help someone to track you down to reunite you with your belongings. I recommend putting only your name and phone number on your luggage tag; there's no need to provide your home address to strangers, letting them know that you're not at home.

- Avail yourself of the plastic laundry bags in hotel rooms to store laundry as you travel. You can also keep a few extra plastic bags in the outside pocket of your luggage for emergency purposes. They take up no room, add no weight and can truly come in handy.

- Perhaps you will want to keep at the ready a travel bag of items that must go with you on your travels, containing travel-size deodorant, toothpaste, lotions and so on. You can grab it and go and know you have what you need.

- If you haven't exceeded the weight allowance for your bag, pack a lightweight duffle bag flat in the bottom of your bag. It can be helpful for the return trip to hold any souvenirs you may have accumulated.

Savvy Travel Sites

The following are helpful travel sites to help you research your trip and to be aware of government guidelines.

- **TSA**
  www.tsa.gov/travelers/airtravel/assistant/index.shtm

- **U.S. Department of State**
  www.travel.state.gov/travel/tips/tips_1232.html

- **Frommer's**
  www.frommers.com/tips
- **Flying with Kids**
  www.flyingwithkids.com
- **Travel Channel**
  www.travelchannel.com
- **Travel and Leisure**
  www.travelandleisure.com
- **Magellan's**
  www.magellans.com/store/travel_advice
- **Weather**
  www.weather.com
- **Currency Converter**
  www.oanda.com/currency/converter
- **Online Language Translation**
  www.babelfish.yahoo.com

"We live in a wonderful world that is full of beauty, charm and adventure. There is no end to the adventures we can have if only we seek them with our eyes open."
—Jawaharlal Nehru, former Prime Minister of India

By implementing the tips and techniques described in this chapter, you will be able to travel confidently, knowing that you have packed and planned in such a way that you will look your absolute best and will have all you need at your fingertips. By eliminating the stress of packing, you can enjoy your travels. Now that you have a good overview of how to be a savvy traveler, all you have to do is decide where you want to go.

ADENA DITONNO
adenaDesigns

(415) 729-1008
adena@adenadesigns.net
www.adenadesigns.net

Adena began her professional career as a Product Marketing Manager for a dermatological company in Northern California. After successfully launching and managing the company's first two products, she moved into healthcare advertising as a Senior Account Executive, working with clients such as Amgen and Dey Laboratories.

Adena parlayed her love of fashion and style into a wardrobe and image consulting business in 2003 when she founded adenaDesigns. She loves helping women discover and embrace their own individual styles. Adena conducts closet audits and wardrobe analysis, does personal shopping to fill in the gaps, and writes a monthly *Style Bulletin* to help her clients stay abreast of the latest information in the world of fashion. She also writes a local fashion column in the monthly newsletter in her community. Adena is an independent consultant for JanaKos Collection, a high-end designer line out of New York, and has organized and participated in many fashions shows over the years to help nonprofit organizations in their fundraising activities.

Adena lives south of San Francisco, and is a member of the Board of the Association of Image Consultants International, San Francisco Bay Area chapter.

International Departures— Domestic Arrivals
Shopping the World for Your Unique Look

By Lena Piskorowski, AICI FLC

There are many different elements that go into getting dressed and dressing well. There is the fit, the appropriateness of the outfit, the occasion, the accessories, how you want to be perceived, the mood you're in and so on.

Custom clothes are a large part of my business, and I outfit many of my clients in this type of apparel. Aside from excellent fit and being able to control exactly how the garment looks, people are most excited about being *different*. There is a feeling like nothing else, to know that what you have on is uniquely *you*.

"In a world where everything is a copy, YOU remain an original."
—Author Unknown

Another way to set yourself apart and really make an outfit feel special to you is to buy while traveling. This ensures that your wardrobe is truly a "collection" of your life instead of a vault of a few specific brands. Also, it is terribly hard for someone else to mimic the alligator clutch you bought in an open market in Tampico, Mexico, especially if you purchased it 20 years ago and the artisan who made it is no longer in business.

In this travel-inspired chapter, you will learn how and why people dress the way they do in various cities. This will help prepare you for your next trip, whether for business or pleasure, or for that cross-country move. Knowing what else is out there will also inspire you. You can borrow elements that you would love to wear and create your own style.

You will also learn how to be an educated shopper away from home, knowing:

- What to look for
- What to buy
- Where to get it

Dressing the Part

Fashion makes the world seem like a smaller place; it is a universal language. You could be sitting next to a stranger in an unfamiliar city, take a glance at him or her and feel as though you might click with that person. To base this on what one is wearing may sound superficial, especially in the context of dating, but it is true! Our clothes and accessories project our personality, our mood and what is important to us.

Since so much about ourselves is revealed before we even speak, don't you want what you're wearing to represent the real you?

When considering what to wear outside of where you live, most peoples' biggest fear is looking like a tourist and being ill-prepared. Living in San Diego for example, you may not own a pair of rubber boots or an umbrella. However, you might want to bring both to accommodate the frequent, yet short, rainfalls you will face on your trip to London.

Whether you want to blend in or simply make sure you are well-prepared, here is a cross-continental dress code to give you a broader perspective. The summer months are the easiest, not only to pack for (less bulky clothing) but also to plan for. Whatever you usually wear in the summer will work wherever you intend to travel in the United States. Confusion can start to kick in when traveling to those areas that have more than one season, especially if you are not familiar with the climate.

A basic point to remember: the farther west you go, the more colorful and casual the form of dress. While virtually every city has its own versions of a creative neighborhood, business district and upscale area, these general guidelines are meant to help prevent you from wearing open-toe shoes in the snow or getting sock tan lines at the beach.

San Francisco

You might be surprised: Just because it is on the coast and is in California, does not mean that San Francisco is a sunny beach town.

This city has a "fall-like" climate for most of the year. Its foggy days and chilly breezes make a jacket and a lightweight scarf essential. You do not need anything heavy here; a blazer or a lightweight jacket will work well. Check your itinerary and dress accordingly. If you will be biking on the Golden Gate Bridge, I suggest wearing something warmer than you would wear to wander around Fisherman's Wharf and the Marina District.

Los Angeles

You might be surprised: While it seldom rains or falls below 50 degrees, you will not be wearing beach gear the entire year.

Summers here extend into the typical fall season, and the occasional "beach day" weather has been known to pop in and out throughout the year. No heels on the strand! The beach culture is too laid back for that. Save the minidresses and stilettos for your nights out in Hollywood. Since L.A. is home to many denim brands (Citizens of Humanity, Rock & Republic, True Religion), jeans are taken seriously.

Denver

You might be surprised: One day it may snow several feet and the next, be sunny and 70 degrees.

The Rocky Mountains in your back yard means you could, if you're up for it, partake in an outdoor activity at a moment's notice. In this rugged, yet artsy city, you will be hard-pressed to find a suit amongst business people. It is best to dress in thin layers to be ready for a cool evening or a sun-powered afternoon.

Especially in the resorts, you can have fun experimenting with an alpine look during the winter. Outfit yourself in fur, shearling, fleece and the latest material in outdoor apparel.

Do not let the lack of ocean deter you from wearing sunscreen or staying hydrated; you are always at least a mile above sea level!

Chicago

You might be surprised: Heavy fabrics will hurt, not help, during the winter months.

The lake effect provides bitter temperatures, but that does not mean that piling on the clothes and looking like a snowman is the answer.

In a city most commonly tackled on foot, wearing heavy fabrics will only result in your being hot and bothered. Instead, having a quality wool coat will enable you to wear thinner fabrics underneath and stay comfortable. As Chicago is more conservative than the cities to the West, in the summer months, men should avoid sandals and shorts at nicer restaurants, many of which have dress codes. Bags are an important accessory here. Make sure yours is large enough to fit the day's needs, but small enough for you to carry from morning 'til night without wanting to cut off your arm!

New York City

You might be surprised: Blending in here is easy.

Part of what makes the United States so interesting is the people who make up this country. There is not a place that better reflects our diversity than New York City. New Yorkers are a little more put-together than most, so bring it up a notch here. Structured silhouettes take precedence over the bohemian vibe of warmer climates. The overall feel is sleek, so bring out the classics. When in doubt, wear black. Boots of every shape and size are ideal to have, especially flat, comfortable ones, as you may be doing a considerable amount of walking. If the temperature is warm, pair them with a dress; if the weather is colder, wear them with jeans or trousers.

If you are anxious about the dress code in the Big Apple, read up on the latest trends in magazines so you will know what to expect.

Remember, except for most business environments, jeans and a stylish top make an easy go-to look you can wear anywhere.

Global Glamour

Clothes and accessories have sentimental meaning. Look in your closet. Better yet, look at what you have on today. Chances are strong that a piece of your outfit reminds you of something or someone—of the day you bought it, the feeling you had when you received it or where you were at that time in your life.

I have a friend who had her grandmother's front door shipped from Dubai to her home in Los Angeles, where it then housed her television. Could she have bought an Old World-looking television stand from Restoration Hardware®? Probably. Would it have cost less? Possibly. To her, the meaning of that piece of furniture and the fact that no one else would have it was worth the effort. Personal meaning and uniqueness—that is what an eclectic look, whether for your own appearance or for that of your home—is all about.

What to Look For

Inspect the details. Attention to detail equals quality. Items made with care will look more elegant and will wear better in the long run.

Soft goods. If something is embroidered, make sure the thread is tightly woven. Look inside the garment; is there an appliqué backing behind the embroidered area? (That is the patch on the inside of the decoration.) If so, the embroidery was done by a machine and there's a good chance the appliqué will rub against your skin and cause irritation. Are there beads or embellishments? Also check the inside—there should not be any hanging threads—all should be sewn down. Take note of the print, does the pattern match up at the seams? Look at the hem, too. If there is a lace trim along the inside, it is a quality-made piece, one that will lay nicely when you wear it.

Hard goods. Handbags should have reinforced stitching on the handle. Contrast lining inside (satin or patterned cotton are popular options) shows more craftsmanship; it's all in the details.

I recommend expensive purchases be in solid colors, whether you are buying trousers, shoes or handbags. Black, tan, white and other neutrals make these good investment buys. Spend less on the embellished and colorful items. You will get less use out of them.

Check the material. Blended fabrics will wrinkle less and are durable. Pure material is more expensive to source and usually has a softer hand to it—think baby cashmere. When checking the label, if you see an ingredient that is unfamiliar, chances are it is a man-made material and I suggest you not pay top dollar for it.

Think about how you will wear the piece and quickly estimate the cost per wear (the price divided by the number of times you expect to wear it). Remember, items in lightweight fabrics can easily be worn layered with other clothes. Bikini wraps can be worn as scarves or vice versa.

Any type of fur, leather or animal skin (such as python or crocodile) is going to be an investment worth making. Not only do these pieces provide an added "pop" to any outfit, every few years they come back around in some form of the latest trend. When they are not "in" you can stand out and come across as someone too stylish to follow fads! In addition, because size is not a concern and these materials last (almost) a lifetime, you can pass these on to someone in your family—a gift to remember. *Note: Be sure to check customs regulations and endangered species laws before you purchase animal skins or products.*

Many people do not think to do this, but buying material abroad and having it made into something when you return home is an excellent way to have a one-of-a-kind dress, suit or decorator pillow, for example. As a resource, remember these are the masters in materials because of their geographic location and skilled labor:

- China: silk

- Italy: wool

- Korea: knits

I still wear a pair of white linen trousers I bought from a market in Florence, Italy, eight years ago. They are a perfect summertime classic. Although they are not always part of the "on trend" rotation, if something is well made and constructed from quality material, it will not go out of style. Buy it and hold on to it.

Can these unique pieces be bought in other areas besides their native lands? Of course! Now more than ever you can have a free-trade bracelet made by tribal women in Zimbabwe or a woven bag direct from Morocco. Online opportunities can provide you with a vast selection of goods from around the globe.

Where to Get It

Limit the megastore visits. This is about going off the beaten path and finding a treasure, not going into Old Navy® in San Francisco or H&M® in Sweden. If a store is not available in your town, I understand the need for your visit. However, if it does exist where you live, then stick to new shops where you may be pleasantly surprised. Sometimes the best is found where you least expect it.

A colleague of mine from London was very excited to check out the Anthropologie® store when she came to visit Southern California.

I found it odd. London is known for its impeccable tailoring and numerous shopkeepers. Why the excitement for an American chain? Because she did not have access to it in the U.K.

Avoid the Louis Vuittons, Guccis, Rodeo Drives and Michigan Avenues of your destination. Even if you can afford a shopping spree at these designer stores or on these famous streets, you will not find anything culturally distinct or specific to the region; you are not setting yourself apart here.

> *"The element of unpredictability should be*
> *part of the adventure of shopping."*
> —Joseph Epstein, American essayist and editor

We are aiming for bits and pieces that really make you smile, something to help you remember your trip. Once when I was traveling in Prague, the weather unexpectedly turned very cold. Instead of strolling along a neighborhood street, I had to shop out of necessity. I popped into the nearest store and bought a pair of jeans with seams all over them. They were unique at the time, ugly when I think about it now.

Are jeans an extremely different find? Is this a quality piece I can pass down to my family? No. I don't even know where those jeans are anymore! However, I do still remember laughing hysterically with my travel mates as we tried everything on at the store while trying to communicate in Czech. That, to me, made the purchase worthwhile.

If a trip abroad is not in your near future, try these spots in your own backyard for elements to add to your style.

Vintage and consignment shops. Many stores in these two categories specialize in specific decades (the '20s, '40s or '60s) or types of merchandise (handbags, concert tees).

Garage/yard/estate sales. As my grandfather used to say, "One man's junk is another man's treasure."

Roadside vendors. You will often see these when you are driving throughout the United States, particularly in the Southwest, where you can find some wonderfully crafted Native American pieces. There is also a large amount of touristy nonsense, so have a keen eye.

Gem and jewelry shows. These shows are especially fun if you are talented enough to make your own jewelry or know someone who can. Along with being able to buy precious gems at discounted prices, there are also a myriad of loose beads and stones you can use to create your own accessories.

Art festivals, DIY (Do-It-Yourself) shows and antique markets. These are more often good resources for interior decorating.

With all of these sources, make sure the items you are buying are clean and in good condition. Sure, a hose and a fresh coat of paint can turn an old shelf into something very chic, but a floral muumuu from the '70s? Just because something is old does not mean it is valuable.

You can run around the world, dine on exotic cuisines, socialize with different kinds of people, and after it all, you come home—however temporary or permanent that is for you. Travel and the adventure of experiencing other lifestyles is an excellent opportunity to add to your look and to create a style that is uniquely yours and not easily copied. Training your eye to know what to look for and where ensures you will buy quality pieces that can last a lifetime.

LENA PISKOROWSKI, AICI FLC
Wardrobe Stylist

DRESS . . . for who you want to be.

(310) 880-8343
lena@dresslp.com
www.dresslp.com

Lena Piskorowski is the founder of DRESS, a fashion consulting company. As the granddaughter of Detroit dressmaker Aniela Piskorowski, Lena grew up surrounded by fabrics, patterns and women chatting as they were fitted for their couture clothing. She knows which materials are the least forgiving, what styles look best on different silhouettes and how the length of your skirt can do wonders for your look!

A regular fashion columnist and style contributor, Lena is known for her witty and down-to-earth take on what's hot, what's not and why you shouldn't stress about it. A frequent traveler with a knack for finding the unusual, she loves to share her favorite shopping finds and destination secrets.

Before launching DRESS, Lena worked with Fortune 500 companies on their brand identity through custom apparel, employee uniforms and private labeling. Certified through the Body Beautiful Institute and a member of the Association of Image Consultants International and Fashion Group International, Lena counts among her clients entrepreneurs, professional athletes and those wanting a fresh start.

Smart Social Strategies
Do Life with Style

By Kimberlee Jo Buckingham, MBA

***Smart is the new perfect. Being smart is sustainable.
Being perfect is not.***

Like many women, I spent most of my life trying to be perfect. To me, "perfect" meant not only having style, but also measuring up to other people's expectations—at least my perception of their expectations. Of course, "perfection" is impossible. Letting go of the drive to be perfect was the first step in my development of a philosophy I call Smart Social Strategies. I have learned that having style means developing an authentic and inspiring presence, a well-deserved positive reputation and self-respect.

Our world has evolved into a global, interconnected, multi-generational, multi-cultural environment—and American culture is constantly changing as we adapt to various influences. We are so fortunate to live and work in diverse communities. However, navigating a culturally diverse social environment with style can be challenging. How do we adapt to rules and norms we may not even know? *The key to being stylish and smart is acting with honor and grace.* The values of Smart Social Strategies—presence, honesty, creativity, sincerity, and strength of character—speak to individuals of all cultural and social backgrounds.

Smart Social Strategies provides a methodology for cultivating these traits. It begins with a solid understanding of basic etiquette and proper behavior. The smart woman chooses how to use that knowledge in each interaction while accounting for the context and the backgrounds of others. She is a woman who is thoughtful, understands etiquette and how to apply it, and reacts with grace. She has style!

Applying Smart Social Strategies in today's society will provide you with the tools to exude humble confidence, savvy professionalism and class—key elements of a stylish life. The "Smart" philosophy starts with the following five steps:

1. Stop and think about your approach

2. Master the basics

3. Authenticity

4. Reality check

5. Thoughtful action

You do not have to be perfect; you do not have to be brilliant; you simply want to be smart. The foundation of Smart Social Strategies is the Golden Rule: "Do unto others as you would have them do unto you." Applying this philosophy to our current global culture will drive results. And here's the best part: Smart Social Strategies are sustainable.

The SMART Steps

1. Stop and Think About Your Approach
At this unique time in history, our society comprises four generations operating in a multi-cultural, multi-lingual, global economy. Having

style means being able to adapt one's approach according to the ages, backgrounds and cultural differences of others. Achieving your goals is easy when you take into consideration what you want to accomplish, who your audience is and how best to communicate in order to reach your goal. For example, when you are conducting a meeting with individuals whose ages vary greatly, demonstrate etiquette so that the silent generation and the baby boomers feel respected, and keep the overall style of the meeting more casual in order to keep the Gen Xs and Ys engaged and contributing their ideas.

In a multi-lingual, multi-cultural business discussion, speak clearly and explain the concepts so that each person understands and can contribute. This is not only respectful; it maximizes the value of the meeting.

"Excellence is an art won by training and habituation. We do not act rightly because we have virtue or excellence, but rather we have those because we have acted rightly. We are what we repeatedly do. Excellence, then, is not an act but a habit."
—Aristotle, Greek philosopher

This adaptation is simply a matter of considering the expectations and comfort levels of various individuals and accommodating them equally. This conveys respect that will earn and deepen relationships.

2. Master the Basics
Know the fundamental societal and cultural norms and apply them. Take the time to learn social and business etiquette, as well as behavior expectations for the workplace, networking and social

media. There are many highly-respected etiquette schools in the United States that offer various levels of training. Becoming comfortable with the rules of etiquette allows you to be at ease in a variety of environments and display your true personality. For example, when you need to introduce the president of your organization to your top client, knowing proper business etiquette demonstrates your ease and your professionalism. If you attend a dinner with senior level executives, use proper dining etiquette. Keep the executives' focus on you and your content, not on your manners. Knowing how to conduct yourself instills self-confidence and humble swagger.

Breaking the maxims of our overly casual society demonstrates that you have style with a twist: Offer your seat on the airport tram to an elderly person; wait until everyone is served before you begin eating; look a new acquaintance directly in the eye while shaking hands and pay her a compliment. You will be pleasantly surprised with the results you achieve when you take the time to pay attention to others. Understand that, because of the myriad variations in people and circumstances, it is impossible to handle all interactions perfectly. The goal is to be smart, not perfect. When you have earned a reputation for style and authenticity, others will readily overlook minor faux pas. The benefits of acting with style will fill your spirit and build your presence.

3. Authenticity

When we move away from our center, where our core values exist, we experience an uneasiness that affects our outward behavior. We may seem "fake" or untrustworthy. Honor your feelings and be true to yourself. Ask yourself whether or not you are truly comfortable with an action or decision. Do you sense doubt, or that little feeling in your gut that tells you to reconsider? Listen to that little feeling.

> *"When you get what you want in your struggle for self*
> *And the world makes you queen for a day,*
> *Just go to a mirror and look at yourself,*
> *And see what that woman has to say . . ."*
> — from the poem, The Woman in the Glass,
> adapted by an unknown author from The Guy in the Glass,
> written in 1934 by Dale Wimbrow, American writer

I once worked for a multibillion-dollar, fast-growing company that offered the opportunity for significant financial rewards. Often, I would lock myself in a stall in the ladies' room and cry because of the rudeness I encountered from my colleagues. In the company culture, making the deal was much more important than treating people with respect. I found myself becoming taciturn, demanding and increasingly unhappy. I was losing touch with my core values, which made me cranky with my family and disappointed with myself. Looking around at my successful colleagues, I thought, "I do not want to become the kind of person they are," so I resigned and joined a company with values more congruent with my principles. If you are genuine, credible and dependable, people will recognize your style and feel drawn to you. It is worth it to live an authentic life.

4. Reality Check
Think about how others will perceive and react to your actions. Objectively assessing how your actions will look and feel to others—regardless of your intent—takes practice.

When I was working for a global software company, I had an experience that reinforced the significance of acting wisely. My team was presenting a software application demonstration for our largest customer in the region. Of course we were all nervous. At our morning coffee break, the sales manager harshly criticized the system engineer for making a mistake during the demo. One of the customers witnessed this, unbeknownst to anyone on our account team.

The next day, I called the customer's Chief Information Officer to discuss our next steps and he informed me that they would not be working with us. I asked to meet with him and he told me the story. I apologized profusely and worked very hard to win the customer back by embodying my own style. I conveyed professionalism and respect throughout the entire sales cycle. I was punctual, sent thank you notes, brought flowers for the administrative assistant and tried hard to clearly understand and respond to their needs.

> *"Seek opportunities to show you care.*
> *The smallest gestures often make the biggest difference."*
> —John Wooden, American basketball coach

In retrospect, taking the time to notice the little things and show how much their respect meant to me helped me earn their trust to do business. By consistently applying the customer's reality to the methodology, you can have great results.

5. Thoughtful Action

Living a life of style means acting with grace. Grace is accepting other people's flaws as well as their gifts. It is responding to challenging situations as constructively as possible. This does not mean you must accept consistently poor behavior from others; rather, it means recognizing that we all have occasional lapses in judgment and temperament. While most people have good intentions and try their best, they may disappoint you—whether in business, social or personal relationships. When a colleague barges in on your conversation with your best client, or when one of your team members displays terrible table manners in front of the CEO, be smart about how you react. Remember the Golden Rule and apply it. These situations may be opportunities to enrich a life with thoughtful mentoring. Challenging interactions may be opportunities to demonstrate sustainable class and style. Act with grace and you will leave a positive and lasting impression.

"Don't reserve your best behavior for special occasions. You can't have two sets of manners, two social codes—one for those you admire and want to impress, another for those whom you consider unimportant. You must be the same to all people."
—Lillian Eichler Watson, American etiquette expert and author

Smart Social Strategies Are Good for Business

Faith Popcorn, a respected futurist, trend-spotter and cultural detective, writes in her 2010 Trend Report that people are gravitating toward an ethos of "S.O.S. (Save our Society)" as "the Country rediscovers a social conscience of ethics, passion and compassion." Her business advice: "It's all about relationships. How does the customer feel about 'them'—not 'them' with the big 'T' but 'them' with the little 't'—meaning the person."

As a society, we are craving more meaningful interpersonal relationships. We want people to care. We want to do business with people and companies that are interested in what we really need.

Three powerful businesswomen, Emily Post, Mary Kay Ash and Indra Nooyi, embody the values of Smart Social Strategies, building businesses and achieving financial success by honoring individuals and customers. Compassionate communication is sustainable as is demonstrated in these women's actions as described below. Their successes continue to improve the quality of human life over decades, and are proof that you can apply smart social strategies to make an enduring difference.

In 1922, Funk & Wagnalls published Emily Post's bestseller, *Etiquette in Society, in Business, in Politics, and at Home.* Emily lived and taught the importance of being smart about how you live your life. She once said, "Nothing is less important than which fork you use. Etiquette is the science of living. It embraces everything. It is ethics. It is honor." In 1946, she founded the Emily Post Institute, which continues to teach people how to apply etiquette in all aspects of life with respect and consideration. Understanding the timeless etiquette basics has helped many individuals and corporations achieve sustained success. IBM has worked with the Emily Post Institute to help its sales and management executives acquire that "final polish" to present the professional image for which they are known.

In 1963, Mary Kay Ash invested her life savings of $5,000 to found Mary Kay, Inc. In her autobiography, *Miracles Happen,* published in 2003 by HarperCollins Publishers, she writes, "When I began this company, I seemed to stand alone in my belief that a business could be predicated on the Golden Rule. Now, the Mary Kay family has shown that women can work and prosper in that spirit while achieving great personal success." The company continues to grow by seeking the very best for each person in all business decisions. Senior leadership continues to practice these original principles while driving innovation in products and technology, and setting trends in the marketplace. Mary Kay, Inc. is now a $3 billion company with more than two million independent beauty consultants in 38 countries.

As Chairman and CEO of PepsiCo, Indra Nooyi oversees a $60 billion corporation employing 285,000 people worldwide. During her tenure at PepsiCo, the company has achieved a historic profit climb. In Faith Popcorn's Culture Pulse entry for July 2010, she highlights Indra's success in the context of her commitment to relational rather than hierarchical management, keeping PepsiCo "communicative, transparent and accessible." Indra applies the same relational philosophy to marketing and branding. Understanding that 85 percent of the company's consumers are women, she commented in China Daily that "women usually have a softer touch and more connections with the heart."

Keys to Success: The Results of Smart Social Strategies

As I have developed and refined the methodology of Smart Social Strategies, I have been amazed and humbled by the positive results in my life. I have applied this philosophy to building a successful career, cultivating professional excellence with integrity and staying true to my values. This philosophy gave me the courage to resign from a lucrative job when I discovered that my values were not congruent with the company's values. Yes, I landed another lucrative job with a company where I could be myself. It taught me to take responsibility for my work, to build strong business relationships with colleagues who trusted in my abilities and dedication, and to cultivate the tenacity and self-confidence to close business deals.

The impact on my personal life has been no less gratifying. I have built a strong marriage and close family on a foundation of respect, communication, kindness and acceptance. I have been blessed with strong friendships based on mutual respect and authenticity.

We are lucky to live in our global, interconnected world and to have the opportunity to interact with people of diverse cultures, experiences and beliefs. Conducting business with an amazing variety of people allows you to grow personally and professionally—more than you can dream of. You will have many occasions to use these Smart Social Strategies, which will open new doors of opportunity. Remember the five components:

1. **S**top and think about your approach

2. **M**aster the basics

3. **A**uthenticity

4. **R**eality check

5. **T**houghtful action

As you apply Smart Social Strategies to your life, you will find success, peace of mind and authentic relationships. You are the only person who can change your life to bring incredible success. This is a decade of great opportunity to differentiate yourself to achieve your goals and dreams. Think and act with grace and you will exude style beyond your expectations! *Let's be smart as we live with true style.*

KIMBERLEE JO BUCKINGHAM, MBA
Kimberlee Jo

Do life with style

(503) 880-1496
kj@kimberleejo.com
www.kimberleejo.com

Kimberlee empowers individuals to achieve personal and professional success by cultivating proper etiquette, style and presence. An insightful speaker, she leads workshops for companies, professional groups and women on topics including personal image, presentation skills, interview skills, and social and business etiquette. Prior to launching Kimberlee Jo, Kimberlee had a successful professional career with IBM, Oracle and SAP. She radiates her passion for respect for the individual while working with professionals to achieve excellence. Her blog, www.kimberleejo.com, brings enlightenment about the effects of respect, etiquette and the pursuit of excellence within our global working world.

Kimberlee is certified by the Emily Post Institute and is a member of AICI. Kimberlee holds a BA from the University of California at Berkeley and an MBA from the University of Oregon. She supports the empowerment of women through her involvement in Women Entrepreneurs of Oregon, Dress for Success, Portlandia, The Link for Women and the Oregon Entrepreneur Network. A former Oregon Junior Miss, Miss San Francisco and Dallas Cowboy Cheerleader, Kimberlee has mentored numerous pageant contestants. She shares a 20-acre farm with her husband, two children, two dogs and chickens and loves the urban farmer lifestyle.

A Globetrotter's Winning Style

By Divya Vashisht

Another trip coming up? Yet another suitcase to pack? Facing the same dilemma—what to pack, what to leave? Travel is fun, and better if the destination is abroad. When going on a leisure trip, you can carry what you please, but when traveling for business, following a dress code becomes essential. With the cost of each checked bag shooting skyward, it has become even more important to pack more style in as little space as possible.

You have heard the saying that "fashion comes and goes but style is forever." I'm a very fashion-conscious stylist, and I believe in crafting styles that outlast fashion. I help my clients pack a part of their personality from their closet when they travel. It's good to be "with-it," but it's great to be stylish! Fashion is fun and can be local. Style also speaks a universal language—one that transcends borders and stays with you from one destination to the other with ease.

The above statement is based on my own experience. Having lived and studied fashion in five of the most fashion-forward cities in the world—New Delhi, Mumbai, London, New York and now San Francisco, I have found that the most well-put-together people have one thing in common: an impeccable sense of style.

Every culture and country has a style unique to its customs, traditions and heritage. When we travel, we often face the dilemma of what to wear, especially when we know little about the dress protocol of the country to which we are traveling. Remember the fiasco our favorite fashionistas from *Sex and the City* landed in by dressing inappropriately during their travels to the Middle East? We all live and learn, and a little research ahead of time doesn't hurt.

Having packed for many destinations and observed the styles of glamorous women all around the world, I learned that there is one thing common in all cases—when in doubt, ask! I believe in doing a lot of research on a place and its customs and cultural sensitivities before traveling there.

Dubai. In Dubai, women like all that glitters and shines, gold is their favorite metal and pantsuits in sateen fabric with a touch of glam are acceptable. On the street—actually the mall—is where locals come out and play. In Dubai, girls tote their Louis Vuittons® and saunter in the latest Louboutins®. Carry a pashmina to use as a cover-up in case you find yourself in a traditional souk (outdoor marketplace). Although you will see miniskirts and shorts, they are for people who know the city well enough to avoid the ultra-conservative areas.

China. Here, work clothes are still homogenous suits and ties, even on the hottest summer days. Businesswomen go without makeup and jewelry, and they keep it simple—no display of obscene wealth. On the street, it is advisable to keep your arms, chest and back covered.

India. I grew up in India, which is an interesting dichotomy in terms of ultra-forward-looking versus super-conservative politics. However, when it comes to what to wear and how to look stylish in India, everything goes. While even today a woman in a boardroom is most comfortable in a sari, a pantsuit or a knee-length skirt with jacket is very acceptable, too.

Keeping the weather in mind, choose cotton or linen in summer and some warm jackets for the harsh winter of North India. Accessorize with a colored scarf or some jewelry to keep up with vividly-dressed locals. Do be careful about packing strappy dresses and tube tops. You will be fine in Mumbai, but in the capital city, Delhi, and other parts of northern and central India, such garments may offend local sensitivities. It is okay if you are traveling with your hosts and not stepping out of your hotel, but be extra cautious in any Middle Eastern country about showing flesh as you may end up offending the cultural values of people there.

Japan. I am really fascinated by the Japanese culture, and some of the most stylish and elegant women I know come from Japan. When visiting Japan, think outside the box. Women are advised to wear heels, makeup and a dose of frills, and men must be clean-shaven and have carefully-groomed hair. Pack white shirts when traveling to Japan, as they are one of the most widely-accepted dress items for work.

France. Going for a meeting in France? Please be understated; it's all about blending in there. The French like their culture and appreciate visitors who make an effort to be like them. Choose dark, tailored, unflashy suits—they work for both women and men. When out shopping or doing other touristy activities, avoid bright colors, except as an accent in scarves and other accessories.

To avoid offending the sensibilities of locals, it is best not to wear sport sandals, baseball caps, golf attire, loud logos, sneakers, T-shirts and sexy clothes. In France, it is always best to keep things simple, neutral and classic rather than too trendy or casual.

London. If you happen to go to one of my favorite cities in the world, London, please pack a dark overcoat for winter or a light beige one for summer, even though you will be lost in a sea of these colors. London being London, anything else goes—as long as you have a coat on, it almost doesn't matter what you are wearing underneath. Jokes aside, when in downtown London, wear a suit (and a tie for men, except on Fridays), and if you are the creative type mingling with cool execs, don a uniform of the newest Nikes and skinny jeans.

On the street, London girls throw on a high-low mix of Topshop®, H&M® and Whistles®; they are freer and less polished than other city style-setters. Men wear pegged trousers in primary colors with plaid shirts or tees. Don't opt for chinos and polos—the preppy look won't fly in London.

The United Kingdom has the reputation of being conservative when it comes to fashion. Thanks to the Royal Family, we still get to see very sharply dressed men (Princes Charles, William and Harry), and London also is home to eccentric designers like John Galliano, vintage queen Vivienne Westwood and the late Alexander McQueen. Their designs are absolutely adored by the British and the rest of the world alike. I mention this because some outsiders have a certain image of the United Kingdom as being traditional and stuffy, especially when it comes to business wear.

I remember when I was job-hunting in London, every time I would get an interview call, I would panic about what to wear. I bought all the episodes of a popular TV show, *What Not to Wear,* and followed the advice of the ladies on the show religiously.

Old adages such as "no brown in town" would make me think twice before reaching for my favorite brown heels. I soon found out such rules are as antiquated as men in top hats and penguin suits and women in crinoline dresses. Since it rains so much in that part of the world, it only makes sense to wear shoes that do not show slush and dirt, so yes, you can go with brown. Having said that, remember that Britain is not as relaxed as San Francisco, where you can go to work in jeans and a tee. Feel free to carry your best-fitting suit and matching brown shoes.

Do Your Homework

It's a good idea to ask hosts or business associates for advice on the local dress code. I remember an incident that was a good lesson on the subject. Some years ago, I was in Bangladesh (East Asia) for work, and one evening I decided to go shopping. I had heard a great deal about all the wonderful inexpensive cotton and surplus top designer deals in the capital city, Dhaka. I asked my photographer to come along and we took a rickshaw to get to the old city from the hotel. On the way there and in the market, I noticed a lot of people staring at me. I found that odd, and as I looked around, I discovered I was the only woman in sight. I went to a shop and asked the owner if women were not allowed in that part of the city. He told me that women rarely visited that area and those who did dressed more sensibly. I was surprised at the comment, as I was very modestly dressed in a short tunic top with wide-legged trousers.

My first mistake was the length of my tunic top, which was way above my knees. The most acceptable length in that part of the world is knee-length tunics or kurtas for men and women. My second mistake was that I did not cover myself with a scarf or a shawl, which is one of the biggest cultural faux pas you can commit there. On top of this, I was embarrassed and had to cancel my shopping trip and head back to the hotel empty-handed. Although I learned my lesson the hard way, it was a valuable one.

Packing in Style

Once you have done all your research, it's time to pack your style essentials. There is one thing of which you can be sure: there is no place in the world that has any restrictions on accessories. Stock up on tons of accessories when you next travel.

Let's talk about certain universally accepted clothing items and accessories that are easy to find, pack and wear, starting with what to wear on the plane. Globetrotter divas travel in style and are well put together, head to toe. Let's start with shoes. Due to strict security checks at all airports, it is most sensible to wear shoes that come off easily. Please pack those lace-up sneakers in your checked luggage. It's important to be comfortable on long flights, but sneakers seldom are a sensible option—taking them off at the security check or on the plane to wiggle your toes and stretch your feet is cumbersome. Think wedges, which are comfortable yet stylish. If you are not comfortable traveling in heels, I suggest you get those super cute, super smart ballerina flats. Designers like Tory Burch have revived those little numbers for the feet. You don't have to go designer, just get metallic or a neutral color such as a brown, tan or black—all are versatile and wearable. Either of these styles will also work with most of the outfits you'll pack.

I see a lot of women at various airports around the globe in their sweats—track pants with a big, bold eyeball-grabbing message embossed in shiny or colored paint across the derriere. If you have any of these, please leave them at home. Choose pants in plain, dark, solid colors instead. Team them with a top or tee in a coordinating color.

It's a good idea to carry a big scarf on the plane. It can serve as a third piece to your outfit, which always adds a touch of class. You could choose a jacket for this purpose, but scarves look more elegant and can double as a cover when you want to snooze.

Scarves make for great accessories irrespective of country or culture. I like to play with different lengths, shapes and sizes of scarves, experimenting with various styles of draping and ways to wear them. You can drape one around your shoulders to protect you from the weather and to show respect for a conservative culture, or you can wear it around your neck. One thing I love to do, especially when I am traveling to India, is to drape my long, wide scarves like a sari. It's easy; just follow these steps:

- Take a stole, shawl or a big scarf that goes with the color of your top.
- Tuck one corner into the back left pocket of your trousers, jeans or pants.
- Grasp the other end and bring the fabric around in front of your body and throw it over your left shoulder.

Voila! Your Indo-Western look is ready! You can blend in with women in saris without having to learn how to wear one.

Universally Accepted Style Essentials

I have talked a great deal about what not to wear and what fashion faux pas to avoid. You must be wondering what you *can* wear that looks stylish and works everywhere. Here are some guidelines for packing the kind of items that are accepted and appreciated all around the world.

For a business trip, you have of course packed your meeting clothes according to the dress code of the country you are visiting. Usually, a dark suit with a one- or two-button jacket works fine. You can also add a skirt to the suit. Pack camis or tops in flattering colors.

Invest in a good, long jacket or trench coat in beige, khaki or golden brown. It will work well with most things you will carry with you.

A dark-colored, sporty jacket with three-quarter sleeves can be teamed with most things, such as jeans, a skirt or even a dress.

Do bring casual and leisure wear with you. The easiest and most versatile item you can pack is a pair of great-fitting jeans, preferably in a darker shade.

I also love to combine long, flowing tunic tops with three-quarter-length pants. Find a tunic top in chiffon, georgette, thin cotton or even a knit and team it with khaki, white or black pants. Wear your wedge heels or shiny flip-flops. This is a foolproof look for a dinner party, shopping or a casual meeting that works across cultures all around the world. You can even team up your favorite short dress with a good pair of tights and boots—a look that is stylish and super comfortable.

Now comes my favorite part: jewelry. I am a big proponent and collector of all types of statement pieces. In my collection, I have everything from chunky silver necklaces from India to high-fashion pieces from Club Monaco to designer-look jewelry from stores such as Forever 21®, H&M® and Aldo®. These stores do a great job of manufacturing absolutely gorgeous designer knock-offs—minus the designer price tags.

I always tell people it's better to invest in jewelry and accessories than to keep buying more clothing on sale. If you are a traveler and want to look stylish and make a statement, the safest bets are accessories and jewelry. Carry signature pieces such as a big, bold necklace, chunky bracelets, statement cuffs or cocktail rings. These items can add a touch of your style to anything you wear.

The most important thing to remember is fit. Whatever you pack, make sure it fits you well, enhances you and works with your body shape. Be sure to carry your favorite and most flattering items, and remember, knowledgeable globetrotters have easy-to-manage hair and are well-groomed. Finally, know what works for you, do your homework on the country you are visiting and keep cultural sensitivities in mind. Experiment, mix and match, try an ethnic item or pattern with a safe or solid option. People will forget what exactly you wore, but if you wore it well, they'll remember your style. Keep these ideas in mind and have fun trotting the planet!

DIVYA VASHISHT
Image Consultant/Stylist

(347) 330-7713
info@globetrottersstyle.com
www.globetrottersstyle.com

Divya Vashisht studied image consulting at the Fashion Institute of Technology in New York and personal color analysis at the Image Resource Center of New York. Divya is a co-author in Power Dynamics Publishing's *Executive Image Power,* that was released in 2009. She believes that you don't have to be rich to look like a million dollars.

She's traveled to over 30 countries and visited over 150 cities around the world. Because of her love for travel, she is often described as a nomad by people close to her. She currently divides her time between New Delhi, New York and San Francisco.

Divya is also the writer and image consultant on the TV show *Styloholic* on KCI TV. She volunteers as a personal shopper for Dress for Success.

After working as a reporter, presenter and producer for various media outlets in India (*The Times of India* and *Star News*) and the UK (BBC *World Service*), Divya decided to use her passion for fashion and her people skills to reinvent herself as an image consultant. Her clientele consists of CEOs, highly-placed executives in the media, actors, models and people at crossroads in their lives.

Stop Signs

By Judith Taylor, AICI CIP

We all see them. You know—the big, red octagon-shaped symbol at the end of the road, designed to catch your attention.

They are put there for our protection, to keep us out of danger. Yet, sometimes people ignore them, mindlessly speeding right through. What do you think is on their minds? We have all driven home after a tiring day and realized as we pulled into our driveway that we don't remember the drive home. Scary. Where were our thoughts? They slip away from us and hopefully no one was watching or got hurt.

Just as a lack of awareness on the road is never a good idea, the same is true as you enter your closet. Have you ever thought to yourself, "I can wear this one more season?" "Changing my hairstyle to the one I wore 20 years ago will make me look younger, right?" "I can wear this low-cut blouse that belongs to my teenage daughter—okay, my granddaughter." Most of us travel through the time zones of our life without realizing that both the times and we, ourselves, have changed.

Let's talk. Psychologists tell us we tend to mentally migrate to a time when we felt the most happiness: A time when our self-esteem was high, there was no dieting, we had a cute figure, long, thick, flowing hair, no real earth-shaking concerns. We liked what we saw in the mirror. A tune on the radio can send us back instantly to that time.

That is the past. Let's talk about right now. We have changed, we all do. Let's take the energy from those positive memories and use that to our advantage. You have been there. A class reunion is coming up in a few months. Our first reaction? Panic! We get out the yearbook. Everyone looks so young! We cherish a few memories, and then the worrying starts. Are we doing and wearing the right things to help us look our best?

When an important event—like a reunion, a wedding or your own birthday party—is on your calendar, it is a great time to discover whether you have been paying attention to some of the stop signs that apply to dressing and grooming and explore the possibility of making some changes. Here are some examples.

Let's imagine we take a trip to a shopping center and we start by sitting for a few minutes to visit and sip a cup of tea. We are not waiting long when a woman enters our view. Her stop sign is her hairstyle. It is obvious that she is trying to keep her hairstyle "young." If you saw her from behind, you might have thought she was a teenager. Our first concern is the color. Maybe her hair was dark when she was in her twenties. But this dark? A sure-fire giveaway of a dye job is hair that is one solid color. Most of us have several colors in our hair, and hair coloring by an expert can duplicate this effect. We might skimp in some areas, but not with our hair! We would suggest that she stop and see a hairstylist for a color consultation.

Next we notice a woman in a very short skirt. We guess her age to be over 40. Her clothing is too tight and too short. Our eyes follow her as she goes into a trendy teen shop. She is ignorant of her stop sign, the first commandment of style: Daisy Dukes®—very short denim shorts—are not worn after age 20 unless you have approval from the Fashion Police. Fat chance for most!

Wait, look—here is another woman going past her stop sign. The closer she comes, the more we can see she does not know where to stop with her makeup. Makeup rule number one: foundation should match your skin. She is trying to pull off a tanned face by using darker-toned foundation. She could use a little bronzer over a more natural foundation shade to make it work.

The main feature of her eye makeup is black eyeliner, rimmed all the way around her eyes. Dark-toned eyeshadow colors add years to this fortyish woman. A softer charcoal or brown eyeliner would have been a better choice. Forget the rimmed look. It makes her eyes look like she had been up all night.

With her dark brown hair, this woman could get away with some well-blended, deep-toned shadows, but she might want to save those for an evening out. Her lip color is so pale it makes her look sick. A soft rose would have given her the color and youthful glow she needs. Is that a mole? No, she added it herself with a makeup pencil. Unless you are born with a beauty mark like Cindy Crawford, skip this trick.

Someone new is coming into view. Were her legs in a fire? Nope, it is her hosiery. She is drawing attention to her plus-size legs with rose-patterned hosiery. There is nothing wrong with patterned hosiery on plus-size or petite women, if it is a simple pattern in a neutral color. If you are not a teenager, please pay attention to this stop sign.

Just then, a baby catches our attention. So sweet, but who is that pushing the buggy? Is it the mother? No, it is the grandmother. Some of us are grandmothers at an earlier age these days. This one is 50-plus. The top she has on is low-cut and too short for her body. As she reaches to attend to the baby, there are no secrets left to our imagination. This woman clearly ran past this particular stop sign.

Reality check: No one over 40 needs to show the world her cleavage. This is an attractive woman, and a better-fitting top would cover her tummy, hide the cleavage, and take years away.

Soon after, we see another huge stop sign coming toward us. It reminds me that in Austria recently, some 12-inch stilettos were shown as a fashion first. The shoes we are looking at have four-inch heels. Try to walk in those for a day of shopping and your feet will never take you out again! I notice her shoes and I am riveted by her toenails. They extend beyond her toes about a half-inch and were filed into points. This big stop sign was ignored. Please don't go to this extreme. Keep your feet clean, softened and groomed, and I suggest no more than a three-inch heel.

Here comes a sweet-looking grandmother. Wait, I know her. She is not a grandmother, she is 30. Maybe she was given some of her grandmother's wardrobe? This is someone who is trying too hard to *avoid* the "dressing too young" stop sign. I want you to see the whole picture. Her skirt is a few sizes too big and the hem is way below her knees. The jacket covering a high-neckline blouse is hanging off her small frame. Black "sensible" shoes complete her ensemble.

She is petite, with a slender frame. Her cute shape is hidden. She waves as she sees us. We decide we need a break after all the fashion faux pas and we offer to take our petite friend shopping. She agrees; we duck into the closest department store and start to shop. With the stop signs to avoid in mind, we send her to the dressing room with a few items.

Soon she walks out smiling. "I had no idea clothes could make such a difference." She quickly put her old clothes in a bag, paid for her new ones, thanked us and left. We watch her stroll away with a spring in her step and feel proud. No more stop signs for her.

Now, you understand the stop signs—what to avoid. Let's explore what you can wear to look your best at 40, 50 and beyond. For this, I invite you to imagine you are joining me as we take a look at a client's closet. There's so much black! We might as well be in a funeral parlor. We all love black. Yes, it is a slimming color. How about a little color here? Let us be reasonable. Time to start purging, all the "way above the knees" items go out first. The low-cut tops are next. That leaves us with a way-too-long, sensible LBD (Little Black Dress). What do we have left around which we can build a wardrobe? Still in a plastic cover is a great, youthful-looking, basic black dress with pants to match. Why is this here? She says, "I never wore this."

We are about to bring youth back and kick some age numbers away. She is looking in the mirror with new eyes. The fit is perfect and not too tight. The length—just above her knee—is perfect. You could hear the Hallelujah Chorus coming from her closet.

Now let's add some color pieces to go with the black. She is elated. By adding a few pieces, she can mix and match with joy.

Shoes are little treasures we add as accessories. How can we look age-appropriate and still have shoes to die for? Younger women can get away with almost any style and color, even if they are strapped around her calf, six-inch stilettos in a bold plaid or a neon glass slipper. I want to be trendy, you say. We are not talking AARP here. But if you try any of these, you'll look more like a "Red Hot Grand- mama" than young and trendy. Watch out, a big stop sign is right in front of you. The young do not have veins showing, purple spiders on their calves and calluses from working on their feet for a decade or two. Please pay attention to this often-overlooked stop sign.

Color can cause a big red stop sign. We have all worn red shoes. However, on an older woman, the red color could draw more attention than she would want to bring to her feet and legs.

If you insist on wearing an ankle-wrapped shoe, at least see if it comes in a light or neutral color. Sometimes we can be trendy and beat the odds in brown or black or beige.

The next stop sign is heel height. Again, a young woman can get away with this. Want to have some fun? Let's peek inside a shoe store and watch as the younger women try to walk in the six-inch beauties. Ha! Age has some advantages.

Notice on the talk shows that *only* while they are sitting do we see the hosts with the to-die-for shoes with six-inch heels. I have been backstage, and as soon as the camera fades, the shoes come off. Oh, what we do for beauty!

There is something to be said for staying chic. Nice leather, brown, black or navy is hard to beat. The pump shoe style has been around for years and is not going away. The slingback is such a feminine style. Like the pump, it has stood the test of time. The pump and slingback have no age limit. Have your fun with summertime casual shoes. Just know when it comes to shoes, everyone is watching.

Handbags can be a stop sign for two reasons. First, beware of all the bells and whistles that have been added to some styles. Seems the designers are in competition to see who can put the most bangles, zippers and metal treasures on each purse. Besides being a sight to behold, can you imagine going through airport security with such a bag? Next time you hear an alarm go off, pause and see who tried to carry that purse on board.

Second, consider the color. Brightly-colored handbags are fun and mostly made to go with casual clothing. I suggest a more neutral-colored purse to go with your business attire.

How else can you get around some of these stop signs? If you have great legs and you want to wear a shorter skirt, why not add some tights and knee-high boots? Ladies, all we are advising you to do is tweak your look, just a little.

Older is *not* what it used to be. Today's 50 is like yesterday's 30. Women today are working far into their seventies. Maybe it is the vitamins or the diet or even the gym. Whatever it is, we care about our bodies and it shows!

Looking great doesn't mean looking younger. Styles for ageless dressing can be found in many magazines. Let's take a look at what to wear to look our best at any age. Some of the best tips for dressing and looking great are found in the fit! Make friends with your alterations expert. Keep the fashion simple with clean lines. Go for solids rather than bold, busy prints.

Some of us have reached the age where we have some status. Use that power. We can afford the best and it shows. According to the market research firm NPD Group, women in the 45-64 range spend more on clothing than any other age group.

Quality and fit are a must here. By now, most of us have found a designer who knows what our body needs and we stick to that line for fit and comfort. Think of the basic elbow-length tee. It can be dressed up or down depending on our destination for the day. Here is a spot to put a killer necklace or a silk scarf. Select a white T-shirt or one in a flattering color—the choice is yours.

Jackets are like old friends, ready to blend any outfit together. Fit should always be a must, regardless of which outfit you choose. Besides being a ready standby, a jacket can hide a tummy or a little extra in the hips.

An A-line dress or skirt is nothing new to us. This ageless treasure is a long-time friend that flatters most figures.

Denim is also ageless. When we think of denim, we immediately think of jeans. A great pair or two can add fun to your wardrobe. The most important tip here is to know which style looks best on your body. Slim, boot-cut and straight-leg are styles that flatter us. Keep the pencil-leg jeans for women under 40, unless you are super-thin. The darker the color, the dressier the jeans. Faded and blended colors are considered more casual. A big stop sign is a skin-tight fit. Really, this looks bad at any age.

Lumps or bumps? Not a pretty sight, no matter what your age. And if you have not noticed, let me be the first to tell you—things have moved. Forget the girdles of your past. We've come a long way, baby. Gone are the torture garments meant to suck the life out of us. Now we have soft, clinging, comfortable help. Shapewear is no longer an occasional necessity, it is needed daily. It is the best way to make lumps and bumps go away—temporarily. Trust me, you will want this look every day. For more about shapewear, see Connie Elder's chapter, *The Unseen Essentials of Style,* on page 147.

You know the celebrity who had twins three days ago and is now showing the world her toned body in knits? Trust me, she is wearing shapewear. Fact is, no one would dare walk the red carpet without it.

Speaking of things moving—when was the last time you had a proper bra fitting? If you answered "college," run, don't walk to the closest lingerie store. Most better stores have a trained associate who can fit you with a bra that really works for you. It is amazing how this will improve the fit of your clothes and give you a more youthful silhouette.

One last thought. Thongs! Unless you don't jiggle when you wiggle, leave this to the young and daring. If you have a toned, tight—dare we say—backside, then you go, girl. You make us 50-pluses proud.

Now you know what the stop signs are. Take some time to reflect if there are any you have been rolling past. Once you learn to avoid the stop signs, you will truly enjoy your best style.

JUDITH TAYLOR, AICI CIP
Professionally Yours, Inc.

*It is MY business
to make YOU look GOOD!*

(615) 773-5341
Looknyrbst@stylemanagement4u.com
www.stylemanagement4u.com

Judith Taylor has received noted professional status and certification in many areas of image management and is widely known for her amazing gift for making you look and feel your best. She is an active member of the Association of Image Consultants International, a newspaper columnist and author of numerous blogs and articles. She appears regularly in AICI's *Image Update* magazine and is frequently interviewed on TV. She previously hosted a popular radio show in Nashville where she "helped locals put their best boot forward."

Judith is a sought-after speaker and conference presenter who is talented in her ability to put the audience at ease while delivering information-packed, high-energy presentations.

Serving the greater Nashville area, Judith brings both glamour and style to her clients and operates her business and life with the same philosophies. Do it right! Keep doing it right and clients who come in for a session stay for life. Judith makes it easy, and image management provides all the materials and tools her clients need to continue to look and feel their best.

More My Style, My Way

Now that you have learned many things about how to discover your personal style, the next step is to take action. Get started applying what you have learned in the pages of this book.

We want you to know that we are here to help and inspire you to become your best and most stylish self.

Below is a list of where we are geographically located. Regardless of where our companies are located, many of us provide a variety of services over the phone or through webinars, and we welcome the opportunity to travel to your location to provide you with one-on-one style consulting.

You can find out more about each of us by reading our bios at the end of our chapters, or by visiting our websites, listed below.

If you are looking for one-on-one coaching or group training, many of the co-authors in this book are available to support you. Feel free to call us, let us know you have read our book, and let us know how to best serve you.

UNITED STATES
California
Brenda Azevedo — www.justbcosmetics.com
Adena DiTonno — www.adenadesigns.net
Divya Vashisht — www.globetrottersstyle.com

Colorado
Jana Rezucha, AICI FLC — www.realworldwardrobe.com

Connecticut
Nannette Bosh, CPC — www.bangleandclutch.com

Florida
Cynthia Postula, MA, AICI FLC — www.lookgreatfeelgreatic.com

Georgia
Ronda Anderson, MA, AICI FLC — www.distinguishedimpressions.com

Michigan
Lena Piskorowski, AICI FLC — www.dresslp.com

Minnesota
Dawn Stebbing — www.imageevolutionmn.com

Oregon
Kimberlee Jo Buckingham, MBA — www.kimberleejo.com
Jeanne Patterson, RN, MBA — www.pattersonsignatureimage.com

Tennessee
Connie Elder — www.lipoinabox.com
Judith Taylor, AICI CIP — www.stylemanagement4u.com

Texas
Kim Mittelstadt   **www.kmimpressions.com**

Virginia
Cindy Ann Peterson, AICI FLC   **www.cindyannpeterson.com**

Washington
Monica Brandner   **www.imagebymonica.com**

Wisconsin
Johonna Duckworth   **www.yourcre8tiveimage.com**

CANADA

Nova Scotia
Sheila Dicks, CEG   **www.fashionexpertsnetwork.com**

Ontario
Teca Cameron   **www.tecacameron.com**

Quebec
Randa Mufarrij   **www.randamufarrij.com**

THRIVE Publishing develops books for experts who want to share their knowledge with more and more people. We provide our co-authors with a proven system, professional guidance and support, producing quality, multi-author, how-to books that uplift and enhance the personal and professional lives of the people they serve.

We know that getting a book written and published is a huge undertaking. To make that process as easy as possible, we have an experienced team with the resources and know-how to put a quality, informative book in the hands of our co-authors quickly and affordably. Our co-authors are proud to be included in THRIVE Publishing books because these publications enhance their business missions, give them a professional outreach tool and enable them to communicate essential information to a wider audience.

You can find out more about our upcoming book projects at
www.thrivebooks.com

Also from
THRIVE Publishing™

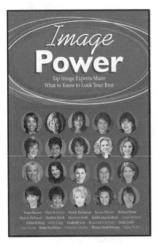

For more information
on this book, visit:
www.imagepowerbook.com

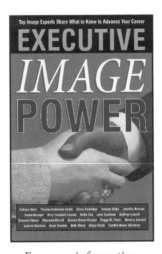

For more information
on this book, visit:
www.executiveimagebook.com

For more information
on this book, visit:
www.execetiquette.com

For more information
on this book, visit:
www.inspiredstylebook.com

Also from
THRIVE Publishing™

For more information
on this book, visit:
www.directsellingpower.com

For more information
on this book, visit:
www.incrediblelifebook.com

For more information
on this book, visit:
www.getorganizedtodaybook.com

For more information
on this book, visit:
www.incrediblebusinessbook.com

For more information
on any of these books, visit:
www.thrivebooks.com

For more copies of *My Style, My Way,*
contact any of the co-authors or visit
www.mystylemywaybook.com